Creating Safe Schools

Students, parents, and school staff deserve a safe learning environment. Yet recent headlines of violence, bullying, and drug abuse have shown the vulnerability of schools. In this timely and important resource, leading expert Franklin Schargel provides leaders, teachers, counselors, parents, and students with the necessary information to address and diminish safety problems in schools. *Creating Safe Schools* explores the background and data about the severity of safety issues facing schools today and also provides the strategies and tools to address them. Clearly organized according to issue, this book allows for easy reference and is packed with tools, activities, checklists, strategies, and tips. Coverage includes:

- Bullying
- Driving and Bus Safety
- Drugs, Alcohol, and Tobacco
- Internet Safety
- Violent School Incidents
- Sexual Activity
- Suicide
- Truancy and Suspension
- Youth Gambling

This important resource will help educators prevent violence from happening in their schools and provide children with a safe and secure learning environment.

Helpful templates and additional resources for educators and parents are available as free downloads at www.routledge.com/9780415734790.

Franklin P. Schargel is an internationally recognized expert, keynote presenter, and training specialist on school dropout prevention. His career spans thirty-three years of classroom teaching and counseling, as well as eight years of supervision and administration.

Creating Safe Schools

A Guide for School Leaders, Teachers, Counselors, and Parents

Franklin P. Schargel

Routledge
Taylor & Francis Group

NEW YORK AND LONDON

First published 2014
by Routledge
711 Third Avenue, New York, NY 10017

and by Routledge
2 Park Square, Milton Park, Abingdon, Oxon, OX14 4RN

Routledge is an imprint of the Taylor & Francis Group, an informa business

Library of Congress Cataloging-in-Publication Data
Schargel, Franklin P.
  Creating safe schools : a guide for school leaders, teachers, counselors, and parents / by Franklin P. Schargel.
    pages cm.
  Includes bibliographical references and index.
  1. Schools—Safety measures.   2. School violence—Prevention.   I. Title.
  LB2864.5.S33 2014
  363.11'9371—dc23
  2013040558

ISBN: 978-0-415-73480-6 (hbk)
ISBN: 978-0-415-73479-0 (pbk)
ISBN: 978-1-315-81971-6 (ebk)

Typeset in Optima
by Apex CoVantage, LLC

Printed and bound in the United States of America by Publishers Graphics, LLC on sustainably sourced paper.

To my family:
Sandy
David
Howard
Pegi
And to my parents, Aaron & Pauline.

Contents

Acknowledgments

Anyone who has written a book knows that even if only the author's name appears on the front cover, many people are responsible for the book seeing the light. I would like to acknowledge some of those individuals.

First, thanks go to my two editors: Lauren Bebe, my editor at Eye On Education, and Heather Jarrow, my editor at Routledge, who polished the work and made it presentable.

I have had the great fortune of having some absolutely brilliant advice from several mentors. To Dr. Marie Sobers and Lori Lamb who I owe more than mere words can express. To my initial mentor, Dr. Myron Tribus who always offered advice and said, "you might want to rethink that." Dr. Jay Smink, retired Executive Director of the National Dropout Prevention Center, and to Lewis Rappaport, my friend and former principal who shaped my professional life, I am in your debt.

Meet the Author

This is Franklin's twelfth book. His first highly successful book, *Transforming Education Through Total Quality Management,* was about how he successfully spearheaded a turnaround of an all-minority high school and reduced the dropout rate of his alternative school from 21.9 percent to 2.1 percent, increased family involvement 1,440 percent in nine months, sent 72.1 percent of its first-generation high school graduates to post-secondary school and raised $5 million for the school. The story has been documented in five inter...   ...eased videos including a PBS spe-
...d articles including in the *New York*

...Solve our School Dropout Problem,
...Director of the National Dropout
...has been recognized by the United
...National Educational Goals Panel
...to help solve our school dropout

...in the United States 171 school
...ever to return. That is our daily
...tion can afford this problem.
...New Mexico and is an interna-
...ut prevention. He is a former
...chool administrator He served
...can Society for Quality (ASQ).
...addresses in forty-nine states
...rope. Two of his books have
...her into Portuguese. In 2005,

the National Dropout Prevention Network awarded him their Crystal Star Award for "Excellence in Dropout Recovery, Intervention and Prevention." He also received the Program of the Year Award from the International Association for Truancy and Dropout Prevention.

The Public Broadcasting System (PBS), *Fortune Magazine, BusinessWeek,* the *New York Times,* the American Management Association, and National Public Radio (NPR) have recognized his work. Mr Schargel was recently nominated for the Brock International Prize for Education for "Demonstrating clear evidence of success in dropout prevention and for retaining students in alternative educational environments". He was one of nine individuals, globally, to be nominated.

Franklin is a keynote presenter, training specialist. He has delivered workshops at local, regional, national, and international levels. Visit his website, www.schargel.com. If you are interested in hiring Mr. Schargel to deliver a workshop or a keynote address, contact him at franklin@schargel.com.

Violence Prevention Quiz

I suggest that school officials distribute this quiz to their staff during a staff development day in order to prepare and make them aware of the need to prepare for safety in school.

The answers to this quiz can be found on the pages 131–133 of this book.

Violence Prevention Quiz: Everything You Thought You Knew about School Violence

The following quiz can be used with staff and parents to create awareness about violence prevention in school.

1 In the 1950s there was a film about school violence. What was its name? ....

2 The "weapon of choice" in schools is ....

3 The "drug of choice" in schools is ....

4 The most deadly school incident in American history took place in ....

5 Schools are safer or more dangerous than they have been in the past? True/False

6 The #1 cause of black male teenage death in America is ....

7 According to the FBI's School Shooter Report, what is the number of students who are afraid to come to school every day? ....

8 According to the FBI's School Shooter Report and the Secret Service's Threat Assessment Report, what do school shooters have in common?

....

9 Do "zero-tolerance" rules against violence or drug abuse work? ....

....

10 According to the US Department of Justice, what percentage of violence against young people takes place in schools? (a) Less than 1% (b) 5% (c) 25% (d) 50%

11 Most school bullying occurs in elementary/middle/high school.

12 Males engage in bullying more than females. True/False

13 Most school violence occurs in elementary/middle/high school.

14 The majority of sexual abuse of children takes place in schools. True/False

15 Most students who carry guns to school do so for personal protection. True/False

16 What percentage of American teenagers has sent nude pictures of themselves electronically? (a) 10% (b) 20% (c) 50% (d) 70%

17 For every hundred people there are .... guns. (a) 20 (b) 50 (c) 75 (d) 90

18 What is the percentage of teenagers who have engaged in oral sex? (a) 20% (b) 30% (c) 40% (d) 50% (e) 66%

19 Gangs exist mainly in urban areas. True/False

20 Girl gang members do not commit crimes. True/False

Introduction

Why Was This Book Written?

Students, parents, and school staff want, need, and deserve a safe learning environment. And schools are supposed to be places where children are safe and secure. Yet recent headlines and media exposure have shown the vulnerability of schools.

What Is This Book about?

In the past, violence, parents believed, was simply a symptom of the inner city. Upwardly mobile parents had the incorrect belief that if they moved to the suburbs, they were leaving school violence, drugs, and gangs and bullying behind. School violence had been happening in inner-city schools for a long time. Some people felt that since school crime and violence were confined to the inner cities and their ethnic populations, it was not their problem. Obviously, many were wrong. Imaginary boundary lines delineating the inner city, suburban or rural communities, whether school or societal, do not stop violence, gangs, guns, and drugs. As incidents in Newtown, Connecticut, Columbine, Colorado, and West Paducah, Kentucky indicate, violence has occurred in rural as well as suburban communities. Who could have predicted a violent school incident on an Indian reservation (Red Lake High School in Red Lake, Minnesota) or in an Amish community (West Nickel Mines School, a village in Bart Township of Lancaster County, Pennsylvania)? Violence has taken place in colleges and universities (Virginia Tech, Oikos College, and the Texas Tower shooting).

No community, large or small, is immune. It is even taking place in foreign nations.

It is not the intention of this book to build on the paranoia built on the Columbine or other school shootings, the tragedies of 9/11, or more recent occurrences. According to Dr. Stephen E. Brock, a professor and the School Psychology Program Coordinator at California State University, Sacramento (CSUS), "violent crimes in schools have decreased significantly since the early 1990s. Not only are rates of school violence going steadily down, but it's clear that schools are the safest place for a student to be." According to the Indicators of School Crime and Safety (2012) issued by the Bureau of Justice Statistics (www.bjs.gov/inde.cfm), "of the 31 student, staff and nonstudent school associated violent deaths occurring between July 1, 2010 and June 30, 2011, 25 were homicides and 6 were suicides. From July 1, 2010 through June 30, 2011, there were 11 homicides and 3 suicides of school-aged children at school." School violence in the US reached a peak in 1993. That year, there were forty-two homicides by students and thirteen "serious violent crimes"—rape, sexual assault, robbery, and aggravated assault—per 1,000 students at primary and secondary schools. The mass shootings at Columbine High School in Colorado as well as the violent deaths at Sandy Hook Elementary School, in addition to the media reports of bullying have reinforced the perception that *public* schools are dangerous places for children. And the presence of metal detectors, security officers, and closed-circuit television systems make school campuses resemble prisons rather than places for learning.

But according to Rob Bligh, a retired lawyer and school board member:

> America's K–12 schools are among the very safest places for a child to be. A child is more likely to die from parental abuse or neglect than to die from all violent causes at school by a ratio of 66-to-1. Parental abuse and neglect kills 1,760 children in a typical year. On average, 26.5 children die each year from all school-associated violent causes.
>
> (http://nepc.colorado.edu/blog/how-safe-
> are-americas-schools January 19, 2013)

Many teachers claim that disruptive discipline occupies up to 50 percent of their instructional time. Teachers discipline the way they were disciplined when they were in school. These techniques no longer work. Increasingly, we are dealing with non-traditional students, who come from non-traditional families. Traditional ways of discipline no longer work with these non-traditional young people. Traditional school discipline is based on the premise, "Do what I say or I will punish you. I will suspend you. I will put you in detention." Do you think this has an impact on children who are beaten, physically or sexually abused? Do you think this has an impact on students who have seen others being killed or injured? Who could ever have envisioned a 4-year-old bringing a loaded gun to school? It happened in Oklahoma City. The boy had to be suspended for one year from his half-day pre-kindergarten program. In Michigan a 6-year-old male killed another 6-year-old first grader in front of twenty-two other students.

Americans in their desire to look for immediate answers seek to identify a commonality to the recent rash of school violence. The one common factor that was identified by the FBI was that most of the communities were unprepared. School violence is not, unfortunately, a new phenomena. In 1955 a film called *The Blackboard Jungle* dealt with school violence in a New York City high school. In the past, school violence was confined to fists and chairs. Today the incidents involve guns (frequently automatic weapons) instead of knives or clubs. In addition, they are taking place in suburban and rural communities involving white or Anglo populations.

Defining Safe Schools

A safe school not only involves gun violence or fighting. School violence takes a variety of forms including bullying and cyberbullying. It involves gay bashing and racial or religious persecution, and suicide. Students are getting pregnant at younger and younger ages. They are using drugs and drinking alcohol.

In a desire to adjust to the perceived increase in school violence, schools have adopted tough zero-tolerance policies aimed at punishing any infraction of school rules. Zero-tolerance policies, which vary widely from state to state and school to school, can seem extreme. A New Jersey teenager, for example, was suspended for five days last year for having an over-the-counter allergy medication in school. And a kindergartner was barred from school for ten days in 2000 for bringing a nail file to class. Initially adopted to combat drugs, alcohol, and violence in schools, these efforts have largely been counterproductive. Stephen Brock of State University of California, Sacramento, cites a study of nearly one million students in

Texas published in March, 2012 (www.npr.org/2012/03/16/148758783/violence-in-schools-how-big-a-problem-is-it) that linked zero tolerance to a surge in suspensions and to higher dropout rates, especially among minorities. When it comes to zero-tolerance policies "there's simply no evidence that they work," he says.

Students bring to class all signs and symptoms of physical and psychological trauma. Serious as the former are (hunger, malnutrition, asthma, and tooth decay), they are no less threatening than the latter (divorce, death, abuse, abandonment, and alienation). And students have nowhere else other than school to react to their situations. The current recession has had a dramatic impact on our nation. Nowhere has it had a greater impact than in the lives of our children in our schools. Teachers must deal with the physical and emotional needs of their students before they educate them. Yet they still need to find the time and energy afterwards to teach the subject matter they were hired to teach. The debilitating effects on educators are cumulative. This may explain why teacher absentee rates are frequently higher than those of their students, and may help us to understand why teachers are leaving the field faster than colleges can train them. Added to this are the deficits that students bring to class because of disruptions in their lives.

Today's young people often live in a fantasy world created by movies, television, and video games. Some of them are optimists. They believe that humans, like cats, have nine lives. They watch people being shot on television and return to work in time for next week's show. They believe that they can extend their lives at way-stations like they can in video games. They believe that they will live forever. Maybe this is why they commit violent crimes.

Some of them are fatalists. They envision that they will die young. Schools are increasingly dealing with growing numbers of angry disconnected youths. They are disconnected from family, school, and society. They are angry about personal things like family divorce, abuse, and breaking up with dating partners. We understand that health care professionals are not miracle workers, but we expect teachers to be.

Who Am I?

I am a former classroom teacher, school counselor, and school administrator who worked his entire professional career in New York City schools. I have had my life threatened in one school, have been stabbed in another. I taught in an inner-city school where over fifty students were killed on their way to school in four years and a student was shot and paralyzed inside the school. I worked in another school where one student stated: "I study in my bathtub at night because it is the only place in my house which is bullet proof." We do not know what challenges our students face when they come to school. After we stopped a student who was carrying a knife from entering our school, the parent told me, "You have it wrong. He wasn't bringing a knife to school. He was taking it out of our neighborhood. In the morning when he comes to school, he walks over bullet casings and dead bodies and at night he walks over crack vials. He needs the knife to protect himself." In my research, most books dealing with school violence have been written by psychologists or psychiatrists. Someone who has been in the trenches is writing this book.

Who Will Read This Book?

I believe that there are three types of people who will read this book. The first type are those people who wish to be proactive and are looking at ways of preventing violence from happening in their schools. The second type of individual is someone who is actively engaged in violence occurring in their building—violence such as suicide, fights, or the formation of gangs. The third type is the individual or group of individuals who has already experienced school violence and wishes to prevent its reoccurrence.

How Is This Book Structured?

A word about how this book is structured. There are several components. The first section provides the reader with background and data about the severity of the problem. The second section will provide educators, students, and parents with activities they can use to address, diminish, and, hopefully, eliminate the problem.

There are a number of tools, templates, and quizzes throughout the book. Additional material has been made available for downloading at www.routledge.com/9780415734790.

The reality is that none of us can ever predict when school violence might take place. But we can do more to increase attention to ways violence in our society can be minimized. And we can take steps to prevent or minimize the impact of those events.

2 Bullying

"Sticks and stones will break my bones, but names will never harm me."
Remember, as children, we used to quote that phrase. Well, as history has
shown, that is not true. Words are very powerful and they can be even harmful.

Kids have been bullying each other for generations. Bullying today is not like it was just a few years ago. The Internet has unleashed meanness to a degree unseen before. Thanks to the accessibility to the Internet and the affordability of new technology, bullies now have multiple ways to harass their victims. The current generation has the added ability to use technology to expand their reach and the extent of their attacks exponentially.

Bullying involves students bullying not only other students but educators and educational staff as well. The bullying of a bus monitor in upstate New York made national headlines because the middle school students posted the cell phone video of the incident on YouTube. There are no data collected on how frequently students bully and harass teachers and other educational officials. And it is not just students who are being bullied. A 2011 study, "Understanding and Preventing Violence Directed Against Teachers," (*American Psychologist,* Volume 68 #2, February-March 2013, p. 75–87) reported 80 percent of about 3,000 K–12 teachers surveyed felt victimized by students, students' parents, or colleagues in the past year. Teachers reported that students were most often behind the verbal intimidation, obscene gestures, cyberbullying, physical offenses, theft, or damage to personal property.

The National Center for Education Statistics (NCES), a branch of the US Department of Education, found that 5 percent of public schools reported that students verbally abused teachers on a daily or weekly basis. About 8 percent of secondary school teachers reported being threatened with injury by a student, as did 7 percent of elementary school teachers.

In addition, students are harassing teachers in what is known as "cyber-baiting." Students irritate a teacher to the point where the teacher takes some action. The reaction is then captured in photos or video and posted online.

Today's school leaders need to arm themselves with new policies and strategies to address aggressive face-to-face or technological behaviors that harm students' wellbeing, their academic performance, and the school climate as well.

Most school bullying takes place in areas that are less supervised by adults, such as on the school bus, in the student cafeteria, in restrooms, hallways, and locker rooms. Schools need to create an action plan to address these spots by providing additional adults to supervise them or using security techniques including closed-circuit cameras. They can also establish anonymous reporting tools like suggestion boxes or cyberbullying hotlines where students can send real-time text messages or leave a voice mail on the school website.

Bullying Background

- The Secret Service's National Threat Assessment Report found that 71 percent of school shooters had been bullied, threatened, attacked, or injured. The report also found that far more shooters had experienced a profound sense of failure or loss—a staggering 98 percent. This included the loss of loved ones or romantic relationships (51 percent) and "loss of status" (66 percent).

- Bullying doesn't simply begin in middle or high school. The Detroit Free Press reported that a 7-year-old hanged himself. The mother reported that her son was depressed because other students were bullying him at his school as well as because of the recent family separation. This death follows the death of a 6-year-old in 2010 in the state of Oregon.

- The US Centers for Disease Control and Prevention reported (in 2009) that 265 children between the ages of 5 and 14 had committed suicide.

- In 1999, only the state of Georgia had an anti-bullying law. Now every state but Montana has one.

- Gay students and special-education students are bullied more than most students.

- Over 50 percent of adolescents and teens have been bullied online, and about the same have engaged in cyberbullying (i-Safe Foundation).

- More than 50 percent of adolescents don't tell their parents when cyberbullying occurs (i-Safe Foundation).

- Girls are at least as likely as boys to be cyberbullies or targets of cyberbullying (Cyberbullying Research Center).

- According to the National Cyber Security Alliance, 70 percent of American parents report that they are the primary source of online safety information for their children, yet 48 percent of them are not completely confident that their kids are using the Internet safely.

- Less than 33 percent of K–12 teachers feel prepared to teach basic computer skills and only one in four feel prepared to teach about the risk of "cyberbullying" or protecting personal information online.

- Cyberbullying targets are more likely to have low self-esteem and to consider suicide (Cyberbullying Research Center).

What Schools Can Do to Prevent Bullying

School-Level and Administrative Interventions

- **Increase reporting of bullying.** Assess the awareness and the scope of the bullying problems at school through student and staff surveys. To address the problem of students' resistance to reporting bullying, some schools have set up a bully hotline. Some schools use a "bully box": students drop a note in the box to alert teachers and administrators to problem bullies. Others have developed student questionnaires to determine the nature and extent of bullying problems in school.

- **Establish a clear procedure to investigate reports of bullying.** Students and parents need to know that the school takes bullying seriously and will take any action, including arrest, to prevent its occurrence.

- **Develop activities in less supervised areas.** In these areas (e.g., schoolyards, lunchrooms), trained supervisors spot bullying and initiate activities such as having roving personnel visit those locations, and having closed-circuit television to limit opportunities for it.

- **Reduce the amount of time students can spend unsupervised.** Because much bullying occurs during the least supervised time (e.g., recess, lunch breaks, class changes), reducing the unsupervised amount of time available to students can reduce the amount of bullying.

- **Stagger recess, lunch, and class-release times.** This approach minimizes the number of bullies and victims present at one time, so supervisors have less trouble spotting bullying. However, supervisors must be mindful that most bullies are in the same grade as their victims.

- **Monitor areas where bullying can be expected,** such as bathrooms. Adult monitoring can increase the risk that bullies will get caught but may require increased staffing or trained volunteers.

- **Assign bullies to a particular location or to particular chores during release times.** This approach separates bullies from their intended victims. Some teachers give bullies constructive tasks, such as tutoring other students, cleaning up trash, and getting involved in sporting activities, to occupy them during release times.

- **Post classroom signs prohibiting bullying and listing the consequences.** This puts would-be bullies on notice and outlines the risks they are taking. Teachers, leaders, and staff must consistently enforce the rules for them to have meaning. Schools should post signs in each classroom and apply age-appropriate penalties.

- **Have high-level school administrators inform late-enrolling students and their parents about the school's bullying policy.** This removes any excuse new students have for bullying, puts parents on notice that the school takes bullying seriously, and stresses the importance the school places on countering it.

- **Provide teachers with effective classroom-management training.** To address bullying, schools should ensure that all teachers have effective classroom-management training. Because research suggests that classes containing students with behavioral, emotional, or learning problems have more bullies and victims, teachers in those classes may require additional, tailored training in spotting and handling bullying.

- **Form a bullying prevention coordinating committee** (a small group of energetic teachers, administrators, counselors, and other school staff who plan and monitor school activities). This committee should develop schoolwide rules and sanctions against bullying, systems to reinforce prosocial behavior, and events to raise school and community awareness about bullying.

- **Hold teacher in-service days** to review findings from student questionnaires or surveys, discuss bullying problems, and plan the school's violence prevention efforts.

- **Schedule regular classroom meetings** during which students and teachers engage in discussion, role-playing, and artistic activities related to preventing bullying and other forms of violence among students.

- **Encourage parent participation** by establishing on-campus parent centers that recruit, coordinate, and encourage parents to take part in the educational process and volunteer to assist in school activities and projects.

- **Ensure that your school has legally required policies and procedures for sexual, racial, and gender discrimination.** Make these procedures known to parents and students.

- **Develop strategies to reward students for positive, inclusive behavior** such as pizza parties, recognition reward certificates.

Teacher Interventions

- Provide classroom activities and discussions related to bullying and violence, including the harm that they cause and strategies to reduce their incidence. Involve students in establishing classroom rules against bullying and steps they can take if they see it happening. For example, students could work together to create the classroom signs mentioned previously.

- Teach cooperation by assigning projects that require collaboration. Such cooperation teaches students how to compromise and how to assert without demanding. Take care to vary grouping of participants and to monitor the treatment of and by participants in each group.

- Take immediate action when bullying is observed. All teachers must let children know they care and will not allow anyone to be mistreated. By taking immediate action and dealing directly with the bully, adults support both the victim and the witnesses.

- Confront bullies in private. Challenging bullies in front of their peers may actually enhance their status and lead to further aggression.

- Avoid attempts to mediate a bullying situation. The difference in power between victims and bullies may cause victims to feel further victimized by the process or to believe they are somehow at fault.

- Refer both victims and aggressors to counseling when appropriate.

- Provide protection for bullying victims when necessary. Such protection may include creating a buddy system whereby students have a particular friend or older buddy on whom they can depend and with whom they share class schedule information and plans for the school day.

- Notify parents of both victims and bullies when confrontations occur, and seek to resolve the problem expeditiously at school.

- Listen receptively to parents who report bullying, and investigate reported circumstances so immediate and appropriate school action may be taken.

What Schools Can Do to Discourage Bullying on a School Bus

- Train the staff (including bus drivers) on what to do if they encounter bullying either in school, en route to school, or around the school.

- Create enforceable rules and inform students and parents of the consequences if children or parents commit bullying. Parents at school games should not be permitted to scream at coaches or referees; if they do, they should be evicted. If necessary, ban their attendance at all school events. Rules that are created need to be enforceable and enforced.

- Rules should be posted in the school, sent home to parents, and put in community newspapers so that everyone is aware.

- All school buses should have closed-circuit televisions so that if violence or bullying take place, school administrators and law enforcement people will be aware.

- An outreach to law enforcement should be made so that law enforcement people are available at the beginning and end of the school day.

- If fights break out on the bus, consider whether law enforcement personnel should be notified and whether arrests should be made.

Cyberbullying

The word 'cyberbullying' didn't exist a decade ago, yet the problem is pervasive today thanks to the use of social media websites like Twitter and Facebook. Cyberbullying is the repeated use of technology to harass, humiliate, or threaten. Mobile phones may be the most abused medium. Bullies send threatening or harassing text messages, often involving sex, sexual orientation, or race. Unwelcome sexual comments and threats of sexual abuse are often directed at girls. Boys are more often victims of homophobic harassment, regardless of their true sexual orientation. Racial slurs and threats of violence are also concerns. In one US study 13 percent of students reported being called a hate-related name.

Email, websites, and screen names in chat rooms are masks for electronic bullies, who can attack without warning and with alarming persistence. Several examples of cyberbullying include:

- Taking humiliating pictures of another student and sharing them with others.
- Verbally abusing another student through texting.
- Spreading rumors about a student on Facebook, Twitter, or Myspace.
- Sending emails or instant messages to their victims.

The consequences of bullying can be serious. Victims' schoolwork often suffers. Some students have dropped out of school, been compelled to seek psychiatric help, and even committed suicide as a result of the distress caused by cyberbullies.

What Teachers and Administrators Can Do about Cyberbullying

- Communicate. Keep everyone affected by electronic bullying informed. Filters for Internet content do not work for most cyberbullying, but helping students combat bullying on their own does. Peer-support and parent-involvement groups also can help.

- Encourage openness. Bullies thrive on secrecy, intimidation, and humiliation. They count on their victims' silence. Openness is a key to reducing or eliminating bullying. Urge students to talk to their parents and teachers.

- Monitor email, Internet, and cell phone use. Responsible adults should determine when students are mature enough to handle electronic communication—especially when such communication may include cyberbullying content.

- Hold bullies responsible. Electronic bullying is a punishable offense. When cyberbullies are identified, hold them accountable. Most schools have anti-harassment policies that should extend to electronic bullying.

- Contact law enforcement personnel to give professional development training to school staff to look for how to identify cyberbullying.[1]

What Students Can Do about Cyberbullying

- Don't engage the bully. Most bullies are looking for a reaction from their victims. Lack of a response can help to extinguish the bullying behaviors.

- Don't share secrets.

- Protect your own privacy. Do not send pictures of yourself on the Internet.

- Think about the consequences.

- Don't respond to and don't forward cyberbullying messages.

- Keep evidence of cyberbullying. Record the dates and times, and give descriptions of what the cyberbully says.

- Report instances of cyberbullying to your parent/s.

---

1 Reproduced from Phi Delta Kappa International P.O. Box 789, Bloomington, IN 47402-0789, USA 800/766-1156, www.pdkintl.org, Share the knowledge. Copies of "Confronting Electronic Bullying" may be made and disseminated (free of charge) without further permission. (© Phi Delta Kappa International.)

What Students Can Do to Stop Bullying

Students may not know what to do when they observe a classmate being bullied or experience such victimization themselves. Classroom discussions and activities may help students develop a variety of appropriate actions that they can take when they witness or experience such victimization. For instance, depending on the situation and their own level of comfort, students can do the following:

- Seek immediate help from an adult and report bullying and victimization incidents to school personnel.

- Speak up and/or offer support to the victim when they see him or her being bullied (e.g., picking up the victim's books and handing them to him or her).

- Privately support those being hurt with words of kindness or condolence.

- Express disapproval of bullying behavior by not joining in the laughter, teasing, or spreading of rumors or gossip.

- Attempt to defuse problem situations either single-handedly or in a group (e.g., by taking the bully aside and asking him or her to "cool it").

Things Parents Can Do if They Believe Their Child Is Being Bullied

- Talk to your child about what happened. Listen to the whole story without interrupting. Be calm and validate what is being said. Remind your child that it is normal to feel upset but it is never all right to be bullied. Ask your child what he/she would like to happen, before you make any suggestions.

- Don't expect your child to solve things on their own.

- Deal with each incident consistently. Never ignore or downplay complaints about bullying.

- Keep a log of the incidents, where the bullying took place, who was involved, how frequently, if anyone witnessed it. Do not attempt to confront the person or their family yourself.

- Contact the school. Find out if the school has an anti-bullying policy. Find out if the school is aware of the bullying and whether anything is being done to address the situation. Make an appointment to speak to a school counselor or school administrator.

- If your child asks to stay at home from school, explain that it won't help and it may make things worse.

- Discuss bullying at school board meetings and with other parents (i.e., PTA).

3 Driving and Bus Safety

Schools have taken on the responsibility of teaching driver's education. In fact in California, schools are required to teach driver's education. A driver education elective course may be applied toward meeting minimum graduation credits without requiring driver education for graduation. Most programs are offered after school, on weekends, or over the summer.

Driving is considered a rite of passage eagerly awaited by 15-year-olds looking for a learner's permit. Children are excited about the feeling of independence that driving affords them. But children are adventurous and do not think of the consequences of their actions. Along with that independence comes responsibility and some children lack the maturity that comes along with the responsibility. Teenagers are involved in more car accidents than any other age group. In fact, teenagers are four times more likely to be killed in car accidents than any other age group (www. lawfirms.com/resources/personal-injury/auto-accident/facts-about-teen-car-accidents.htm). Every day, car crashes end more teen lives than cancer, homicide, and suicide combined (http://teendriving.aaa.com/CA/getting-ready/understand-facts-and-risks)—a total of 3,115 teenagers ages 13–19 died in motor vehicle crashes in 2010 (www.rmiia.org/auto/teens/Teen_Driving_Statistics.asp). Almost half of US students in their last year before college admit they text or email while driving. In 2011, 45 percent of all students 16 and older reported that they had texted or emailed while driving during the past thirty days, says the study by researchers at the Centers for Disease Control and Prevention and reported in *Pediatrics* and *USA Today* (www.usatoday.com/story/news/nation/2013/05/13/texting-driving-teens/2150755/). An anonymous national survey found that 58 percent of students said they had texted or emailed while driving during the previous month. Teenage drivers and passengers are among those least likely to wear their seat belts (58 percent of teen drivers killed in crashes were not wearing a seat belt in 2011, an increase from 56 percent in 2008). See more at: www.teendriversource.org/stats/for_parents/detail/59#sthash. vZVmi0rE.dpuf. See also Box 3.1.

What responsibility do schools have in assuring that the rules of the road are taught and obeyed? Do schools bear any responsibility if children text, drive drunk, high on drugs, or email?

Box 3.1 *Driving Background*

According to the Insurance Institute for Highway Safety (May 2012, www.iihs.org/research/topics/teenagers.html).

1 How serious is the teenage motor vehicle crash problem?

In 2010, 3,115 teenagers (ages 13–19) died in the United States from crash injuries. Such injuries are by far the leading cause of death among people 13–19 years old.[1] The crash risk among teenage drivers is particularly high during the first months of licensure.[2,3]

2 How do teenage crash rates compare with rates among drivers of other ages?

Teenage drivers have high rates of both fatal and non-fatal crashes compared with adult drivers. Teenagers drive less than all but the oldest people, but their numbers of crashes and crash deaths are disproportionately high. Based on crashes of all severities, the crash rate per mile driven for 16–19 year-olds is about three times the risk for drivers 20 and older. Risk is highest at age 16. The crash rate per mile driven is three times as high for 16 year-olds as it is for 18–19 year-olds.[4]

Many teenagers die as passengers in motor vehicle crashes. Fifty-nine percent of teenage passenger deaths in 2010 occurred in vehicles driven by another teenager. Among deaths of passengers of all ages, 17 percent occurred when a teenager was driving.

3 How do crashes involving teenagers differ from those of other drivers?

Analyses of fatal crash data indicate that crashes of teenage drivers are more likely to be attributed to driver error. Teenagers' fatal crashes are more likely to involve speeding than those of older drivers, and teenagers are more likely than drivers of other ages to be in single-vehicle fatal crashes. Plus teenagers do more of their driving in small and older cars[5] and at night,[4] compared with adults. In 2010, 17 percent of teenagers' fatalities occurred between 9 P.M. and midnight, and 24 percent occurred between midnight and 6 A.M. Fifty-five percent of teenagers' fatalities occurred on Friday, Saturday or Sunday.

4   Why is teenage crash involvement so high?

An Institute review of recent literature confirmed that driver age and experience both have strong effects on driver crash risk.[6] Crash rates for young drivers are high largely because of their immaturity combined with driving inexperience. The immaturity is apparent in young drivers' risky driving practices, such as speeding. At the same time, teenagers' lack of experience behind the wheel makes it difficult for them to recognize and respond to hazards. They get in trouble trying to handle unusual driving situations, and these situations turn disastrous more often than when older people drive.

5   How are teenagers' crash rates changing over time?

The number of teenagers (ages 13–19) who died in motor vehicle crashes was 8,748 in 1975 and 3,115 in 2010, a decline of 64 percent. Between 1996, when the first three-stage driver licensing program was implemented in California, and 2010, teenage crash deaths declined by 46 percent (from 5,819 to 3,115). Teenage crash deaths dropped from 3,480 in 2009 to 3,115 in 2010, a decline of 10 percent.

Teenage driver crash involvements per population also have declined since 1996, and the largest declines occurred for 16 year-olds. Between 1996 and 2010 fatal crashes per population fell 68 percent for 16 year-olds, 59 percent for 17 year-olds, 52 percent for 18 year-olds, and 47 percent for 19 year-olds. During the same period, police-reported crashes per population fell 63 percent for 16 year-olds, 51 percent for 17 year-olds, 43 percent for 18 year-olds, and 39 percent for 19 year-olds.

6 What requirements do states have for teenagers learning to drive?

All fifty states and the District of Columbia have graduated licensing systems, although the systems vary in strength. A young driver is first required to complete a supervised learner's period before obtaining an intermediate license that limits driving in high-risk situations until their 18th birthday. Only then can drivers get licenses with full privileges.

As recently as 1995, there were far fewer restrictions on teen licensing. At that time, only twenty-nine states and the District of Columbia required a learner's permit, and only eleven required the permit to be held for a minimum period ranging from fourteen to ninety days.[7]

7 Is alcohol an important factor in teenagers' crashes?

Yes. Young drivers are less likely than adults to drive after drinking alcohol, but their crash risk is substantially higher when they do. This is especially true at low and moderate blood alcohol concentrations (BACs) and is thought to result from the relative inexperience of young drivers with drinking, with driving, and with combining the two.[8] At the same BAC, drivers ages 16–20 are far more likely than older drivers to get into a fatal or nonfatal crash.[9,10] At the same BAC, male and female drivers were equally likely to be involved in fatal crashes.

Among teenage passenger vehicle drivers (16–19 years old) who were fatally injured in 2010, 26 percent of males and 19 percent of females had high BACs (0.08 percent or higher), even though every state has a legal minimum alcohol purchasing age of twenty-one and a zero BAC threshold for teenage drivers. The percentage with high BACs was much lower among 16–17 year-old drivers (15 percent) than among 18–19 year-old drivers (28 percent).

References

1 National Center for Injury Prevention and Control. 2012. Web-based Injury Statistics Query and Reporting System (WISQARS), 2010 fatal injury data. Atlanta, GA: Centers for Disease Control and Prevention. Available: www.cdc.gov/injury/wisqars/index.html.
2 Mayhew, D.R., Simpson, H.M., and Pak, A. 2003. Changes in collision rates among novice drivers during the first months of driving. *Accident Analysis and Prevention* 35: 683–91.

3 McCartt, A.T., Shabanova, V.I., and Leaf, W.A. 2003. Driving experience, crashes, and teenage beginning drivers. *Accident Analysis and Prevention* 35: 311–20.

4 Federal Highway Administration. 2008. National Household Travel Survey, 2008. Washington, DC: US Department of Transportation.

5 Cammisa, M.X., Williams, A.F., and Leaf, W.A. 1999. Vehicles driven by teenagers in four states. *Journal of Safety Research* 30: 25–30.

6 McCartt, A.T., Mayhew, D.R., Braitman, K.A., Ferguson, S.A., and Simpson, H.M. 2009. Effects of age and experience on young driver crashes: review of recent literature. *Traffic Injury Prevention* 10: 209–19.

7 Williams, A.F., Weinberg, K., Fields, M., and Ferguson, S.A. 1996. Current requirements for getting a drivers license in the United States. *Journal of Safety Research* 27: 93–101.

8 Mayhew, D.R., Donelson, A.C., Beirness, D.J., and Simpson, H.M. 1986. Youth, alcohol, and relative risk of crash involvement. *Accident Analysis and Prevention* 18: 273–87.

9 Peck, R.C., Gebers, M.A., Voas, R.B., and Romano, E. 2008. The relationship between blood alcohol concentration (BAC), age, and crash risk. *Journal of Safety Research* 39: 311–19.

10 Voas, R.B., Torres, P., Romano, E., and Lacey, J.H. 2012. Alcohol-related risk of driver fatalities: an update using 2007 data. *Journal of Studies on Alcohol and Drugs* 73(3): 341–50.

What Can Families Do to Prevent Teen Car Deaths

The AAA Foundation recommends that families consider these steps:

- Know the graduated driver licensing system for your state, and remember: even if the law doesn't set a passenger limit, parents can.

- Sign a parent–teen driving agreement that stipulates teens will not ride as passengers of teen drivers without a parent's advance permission.

- Provide transportation alternatives for teens who honor that pledge.

- Talk with other parents so they know the rules for your teen and will help enforce them.

- Spend time as a passenger when your teen is at the wheel. Your presence and your guidance help make your teen a safer driver.

- Visit: Teen Driving (www.theautochannel.com/link.html?www.Teen Driving.AAA.com) for resources that can help teens become safer drivers, including a parent–teen driving agreement covering safety risks like passengers, cell phone use, and night driving.

Driving Contract

A number of private and government organizations and insurance companies are concerned about teenage driving and accidents. They have developed driving contracts to be signed by both parents and students. Schools might want to check with individual insurance companies (Allstate) and the AAA to see if their contracts better suit the needs of their students.

Go into most school parking lots and you will notice that the student parking lot is filled with cars. Many teens feel that the minute they reach the minimum state age of driving, they apply pressure on their parents to either get them a car or lend them the family car. This driving contract delineates the responsibility of the child as a driver and the responsibilities of the parents (see Fig. 3.1).

By having students and their parents sign contracts, they will realize that driving a car comes with some responsibilities as well as a privilege. It might prevent some accidents.

MICHIGAN PARENT—TEEN SAFE DRIVING CONTRACT

We, ... and ...., agree (Name of Teen Driver Names of Parents or Guardians) to the following conditions:

Initial all that apply

TEEN DRIVER'S RESPONSIBILITIES

1. I will not let anyone else drive or use the vehicle entrusted to me.
2. I will obey all driving laws and will drive safely so I will not endanger my life or the lives of others.
3. Everyone in the vehicle will wear a safety belt at all times.
4. I will state my destination and time of return prior to using any vehicle, and I will notify my parents if I think I will be more than 30 minutes late.
5. I will not consume alcohol or drugs or operate any vehicle under the influence of alcohol or drugs.

Figure 3.1 Michigan parent–teen safe driving contract

(*Continued*)

PARENTAL RESPONSIBILITIES

1. I will listen in a respectful manner to explanations or concerns expressed by my teen driver regarding the operation of a vehicle or the terms of the contract.
2. I will provide respectful feedback when accompanying my teen driver in a motor vehicle.
3. I will serve as a good role model when operating a vehicle and coach good driving skills and habits to my teen driver.

DRIVING PRIVILEGES

This portion of the contract may be used to outline any additional conditions or limits on the use of the vehicle as agreed to by teens and parents (i.e., number of passengers, use of cell phone):

_____

_____

_____

_____

_____

_____

(OVER)

OPERATOR IMPAIRMENT AS A RESULT OF ALCOHOL AND DRUGS

A. **Teen Driver's Responsibility.** I will not get into the vehicle of a driver who has been drinking or using drugs. I will seek alternate transportation or I will call you for advice and/or transportation at any hour from any place. I have discussed with you and fully understand your feelings regarding underage drinking and the use of illegal drugs. _____ (Initials)

B. **Parent's or Guardian's Responsibility.** I (We) agree to come and get you at any hour from any place, with no questions asked and no argument at that time, or I (we) will arrange transportation to bring you home safely. I (We) expect that a discussion of such an incident would follow at a later time. _____ (Initials)

Likewise, I (we) as your parent or guardian, agree to seek safe, sober transportation. I (We) will not drive if I (we) have been drinking, nor will I (we) ride with a relative or friend who has been drinking.

_____ (Initials) _____ (Initials)

COSTS AND MAINTENANCE OF VEHICLE

Will be responsible for the following: (indicate dollar amount or percentage of cost)

_____

Name of Teen Driver

Cost of vehicle registration

Check all that apply:

Check oil and other fluids regularly

Clear or clean all windows

Cost of fuel maintenance

Report unusual performance

Refuel when tank is less than 1/4 full

Damage to vehicle

Fines and penalties

Inspect tires and check air pressure

Perform normal maintenance

Insurance costs

Keep interior and exterior clean

Other

_____

Additional conditions or responsibilities as agreed to by teen and parents/guardians:

_____

_____

_____

We agree to the terms of this contract, which may be revisited or revised at a later time.

Signature of Parent or Guardian   Signature of Parent or Guardian

_____   _____

Signature of Teen Driver   Date

_____   _____

Bus Rules

School buses are places where children can be hurt, injured, or even worse. They should be taught the proper rules of good bus behavior and they should be taught it when they are still young. The government of Alberta Canada has developed a series of pamphlets and comic books regarding bus safety for elementary school students. They can be accessed from www.saferoads.com.

Parents and students need to be made aware that riding a school bus is a privilege and not a right. Schools have the ability to exclude children from school buses if they do not follow school rules. Below are some enforceable school rules for students and parents that might be used by schools. Educators can edit them so that they are age appropriate.

General Rules

- Students will be picked up and dropped off only at their assigned stops. The bus driver cannot change the bus route. The driver cannot accept any notes authorizing them to drop off students at a point other than the student's regular stop.
- Middle and high school students are required to show their school identification cards upon request.
- The school bus driver will assign seats to students.

Instructions to Parents

"We want to make sure your child's trip to and from school is as enjoyable as possible. We all play a role in achieving this goal. In order to get your child to school safe, on time, and ready to learn, it's important that he or she understands the school bus safety rules. Please discuss the rules listed below with your child prior to the start of school."

Safety Practices

- Students need to be cautious in the bus loading zone.
- A school bus driver will not stop for students who have missed the bus once it is in motion.

- No glass items, live animals, or dangerous objects will be transported on the school bus.

- Large items may not block the aisle or exits of the bus.

Student's Responsibilities

- Arrive at the bus stop ten minutes before stop time.

- Wait until the bus comes to a complete stop and the doors are opened before approaching the bus.

- Use the handrail. Be careful no clothing or belongings get caught on the handrail.

- Sit in their assigned seat.

- Sit on the seat facing forward, feet on the floor, and speak in a normal tone of voice.

- Follow the driver's directions promptly.

- Keep the noise level down.

- Keep head, hands, and feet inside the bus.

- Don't throw things inside the bus or out the windows.

- No eating or drinking on the bus.

- Keep the bus clean.

- No smoking or tobacco on the bus.

- Don't be destructive.

- Be courteous.

- Cooperate with the driver.

- Stay out of the "Danger Zone"—anywhere within 10 feet of the bus.

- Don't ever try to get anything you left on the bus after you have already gotten off. We'll do our best to ensure personal property is returned.

- Don't try to pick up anything dropped underneath the bus—things can be replaced, children can't.

- Always follow the driver's directions about how to cross the street. Be alert to traffic, look both ways, and always walk in front of the bus.

- The following are things **NOT** to bring on a school bus:
  - Pets
  - Glass Objects

- Skate Boards
- Roller Blades and/or "Wheelie" Shoes
- Sleds
- Balloons
- Toy Guns/Swords (including Squirt Guns)

Discipline Plan

- The principal/designee at the school will address referrals from bus drivers according to their school bus discipline plan.
- The principal/designee has the authority to suspend a student from the bus and determine the length of the suspension.
- Severe disruption and dangerous behavior will result in immediate suspension of school bus privileges.
- All rules listed in the Student Behavior Handbook will apply on the school bus.

Special Needs Transportation

- Special needs transportation will be provided according to terms identified in a student's Individualized Education Plan (IEP).
- Communication between a student's school bus driver and their parent/guardian is encouraged so that the student's IEP plan is implemented effectively.
- Transportation forms must include all information to ensure safe transportation of students.

Bus Safety Rules for Elementary School Students

BE SMART, RIDE SAFE

1 Always be at your bus stop three to five minutes before your bus is scheduled to arrive.

2   If you miss the bus, have a backup plan. Don't take rides from strangers.

3   Wait for the bus in a safe spot at least two giant steps away from the road.

4   Use the handrail when getting on and off the bus.

5   Get on the bus one at a time.

6   Take your seat right away and stay seated until you leave the bus.

7   Sit back in your seat, face forward, and keep your feet to the front.

8   Talk quietly so not to distract the driver. Remember, it's the driver's responsibility to keep you safe!

9   Wait for the bus to come to a complete stop and the doors to open before you leave your seat.

10 After leaving the bus, take five giant steps away from the bus so you are out of the Danger Zone and in a safe spot.

11 Even though the bus might be warm, always dress for the weather outside in case the bus breaks down. Wear clothes that will keep you warm when it's cold or wet outside.

Bus Safety for Parents

Parents and Guardians, especially of young children, may need to be reminded about bus safety rules. Students and their parents should understand that riding on a school bus is a privilege and not a right. Schools might want to establish a set of rules for parents.

Parents' Responsibility

1   Read and discuss with your child(ren) the responsibilities, behavior rules, and violation consequences on School Buses.

2   Inform your child(ren) of the location of bus stop, time, and to wait in a single line.

3   Require your child(ren) to arrive five minutes prior to scheduled time and to conduct themselves appropriately on school buses.

4   Support the school officials in their efforts to operate a safe and efficient transportation system.

4

Drugs, Alcohol, and Tobacco

Why do children take drugs/alcohol? Psychologists, sociologists, and psychiatrists give a variety of possible causes. They believe sometimes it is for the thrill of trying something different. Sometimes it is to "act like an adult." Young people have always been risk-takers. They like to experiment. Drugs and alcohol represent the "forbidden fruit." It may be because they believe that they will live forever so that they take risks that older people would never do. The information in Box 4.1 is quoted from the National Institute of Health http://pubs.niaaa.nih.gov/publications/AA67/AA67.htm.

Box 4.1 *Why Do Some Adolescents Drink?*

As children move from adolescence to young adulthood, they encounter dramatic physical, emotional, and lifestyle changes. Developmental transitions, such as puberty and increasing independence, have been associated with alcohol use. So in a sense, just being an adolescent may be a key risk factor not only for starting to drink but also for drinking dangerously.

Risk-Taking—Research shows the brain keeps developing well into the twenties, during which time it continues to establish important communication connections and further refines its function. Scientists believe that this lengthy developmental period may help explain some of the behavior which is characteristic of adolescence—such as their propensity to seek out new and potentially dangerous situations. For some teens, thrill-seeking might include experimenting with alcohol. Developmental changes also offer a possible physiological explanation for why teens act so impulsively, often not recognizing that their actions—such as drinking—have consequences.

Expectancies—How people view alcohol and its effects also influences their drinking behavior, including whether they begin to drink and how much. An adolescent who expects drinking to be a pleasurable experience is more likely to drink than one who does not. An important area of alcohol research is focusing on how expectancy influences drinking patterns from childhood through adolescence and into young adulthood. Beliefs about alcohol are established very early in life, even before the child begins elementary school. Before age 9, children generally view alcohol negatively and see drinking as bad, with adverse effects. By about age 13, however, their expectancies shift, becoming more positive. As would be expected, adolescents who drink the most also place the greatest emphasis on the positive and arousing effects of alcohol.

Sensitivity and Tolerance to Alcohol—Differences between the adult brain and the brain of the maturing adolescent also may help to explain why many young drinkers are able to consume much larger amounts of alcohol than adults before experiencing the negative consequences of drinking, such as drowsiness, lack of coordination, and withdrawal/hangover effects. This unusual tolerance may help to explain the high rates of binge drinking among young adults. At the same time, adolescents appear to be particularly sensitive to the positive effects of drinking, such as feeling more at ease in social situations, and young people may drink more than adults because of these positive social experiences.

Personality Characteristics and Psychiatric Comorbidity—Children who begin to drink at a very early age (before age 12) often share similar personality characteristics that may make them more likely to start drinking. Young people who are disruptive, hyperactive, and aggressive—often referred to as having conduct problems or being antisocial—as well as those who are depressed, withdrawn, or anxious, may be at greatest risk for alcohol problems. Other behavior problems associated with alcohol use include rebelliousness, difficulty avoiding harm or harmful situations, and a host of other traits seen in young people who act out without regard for rules or the feelings of others (i.e., disinhibition).

Hereditary Factors—Some of the behavioral and physiological factors that converge to increase or decrease a person's risk for alcohol problems, including tolerance to alcohol's effects, may be directly linked to genetics. For example, being a child of an alcoholic or having several alcoholic family members places a person at greater risk for alcohol problems. Children of alcoholics (COAs) are between 4 and 10 times more likely to become alcoholics themselves than are children who have no close relatives with alcoholism. COAs also are more likely to begin drinking at a young age and to progress to drinking problems more quickly.

Research shows that COAs may have subtle brain differences which could be markers for developing later alcohol problems. For example, using high-tech brain-imaging techniques, scientists have found that COAs have a distinctive feature in one brainwave pattern (called a P300 response) that could be a marker for later alcoholism risk. Researchers also are investigating other brainwave differences in COAs that may be present long before they begin to drink, including brainwave activity recorded during sleep as well as changes in brain structure and function.

Some studies suggest that these brain differences may be particularly evident in people who also have certain behavioral traits, such as signs of conduct disorder, antisocial personality disorder, sensation-seeking, or poor impulse control. Studying how the brain's structure and function translates to behavior will help researchers to better understand how predrinking risk factors shape later alcohol use. For example, does a person who is depressed drink to alleviate his or her depression, or does drinking lead to changes in his brain that result in feelings of depression?

Other hereditary factors likely will become evident as scientists work to identify the actual genes involved in addiction. By analyzing the genetic makeup of people and families with alcohol dependence, researchers have found specific regions on chromosomes that correlate with a risk for alcoholism. Candidate genes for alcoholism risk also have been associated with those regions. The goal now is to further refine regions for which a specific gene has not yet been identified and then determine how those genes interact with other genes and gene products as well as with the environment to result in alcohol dependence. Further research also should shed light on the extent to which the same or different genes contribute to alcohol problems, both in adults and in adolescents.

Environmental Aspects—Pinpointing a genetic contribution will not tell the whole story, however, as drinking behavior reflects a complex interplay between inherited and environmental factors, the implications of which are only beginning to be explored in adolescents. And what influences drinking at one age may not have the same impact at another. As Rose and colleagues show, genetic factors appear to have more influence on adolescent drinking behavior in late adolescence than in mid-adolescence.

Environmental factors, such as the influence of parents and peers, also play a role in alcohol use. For example, parents who drink more and who view drinking favorably may have children who drink more, and an adolescent girl with an older or adult boyfriend is more likely to use alcohol and other drugs and to engage in delinquent behaviors.

Researchers are examining other environmental influences as well, such as the impact of the media. Today alcohol is widely available and aggressively promoted through television, radio, billboards, and the Internet. Researchers are studying how young people react to these advertisements. In a study of 3rd, 6th, and 9th graders, those who found alcohol ads desirable were more likely to view drinking positively and to want to purchase products with alcohol logos. Research is mixed, however, on whether these positive views of alcohol actually lead to underage drinking.

What Is the Impact on Schools?

- Drug users have a need to get money. They can get it by stealing from family, friends, or schoolmates.

- Drug and alcohol users encourage, through peer pressure, other students to try these substances.

- Children do not know how to deal with family and friends who use drugs and alcohol and are seeking advice regarding this problem.

- Alcohol abuse leads to binge drinking.

- There has been a dramatic increase in the use of prescription drugs. Children raid their parents' medicine cabinets and arrange, in school, "pill parties." Data indicate this is happening in elementary schools among 4th, 5th, and 6th graders. Frequently, educators do not know the signs of drug/alcohol abuse nor have they established a system for referrals of drug/alcohol abusers.

Underage Drinking and Drug Use Background

- 65 percent of those youth surveyed admitted getting alcohol from friends or family (Century Council, www.centurycouncil.org/under age-drinking/underage-drinking-research).

- Youth who drink alcohol are 50 percent more likely to use cocaine than those who never drink (National Center on Addiction and Substance Abuse 2012 Teen Survey, www.casacolumbia.org/templates/NewsRoom.aspx?articleid=692&zoneid=51).

- Children who start drinking before age 15 are twelve times more likely to be injured while under the influence of alcohol and ten times more likely to be in a fight after drinking, compared with those who wait until they are 21 to drink. (Substance Abuse and Mental Health Services Administration, www.samsha.gov, Underaged Drinking: National Media Campaign Talking Points.)

- Alcohol use by teens is a strong predictor of both sexual activity and unprotected sex. A survey of high school students found that 18 percent of females and 39 percent of males say it is acceptable for a boy to force sex if the girl is high or drunk (University of Ilinois at Urbana-Campaign, McKinley Health Center, What You Should Know About Sex & Alcohol, www.mckinley.illinois.edu/handouts/sex_alcohol.html.)

- According to the Centers for Disease Control and Prevention (CDC) (www.cdc.gov/alcohol/fact-sheets/underage-drinking.htm, Fact Sheets—Underage Drinking), about 90 percent of all teen alcohol drinking occurs in the form of binge drinking which peaks at age 19. Forty-one percent of 12th graders report having had a drink in the previous thirty days, and by the time students are in college the number soars to 72 percent. Approximately 200,000 teenagers go to emergency rooms each year because of drinking-related incidents. More than 1,700 college students die each year from binge drinking.

- According to the CDC (www.cdc.gov/alcohol/fact-sheets/binge-drinking.htm, Fact Sheets—Binge-Drinking), binge drinking is more common among young adults aged 18–34 years. It is also more common among those with household incomes of $75,000 or more than among those with lower incomes. Binge drinkers are fourteen times more likely to report alcohol-impaired driving than non-binge drinkers. About 90 percent of the alcohol consumed by youth under the age of 21 in the United States is in the form of binge drinks.

- Teenage drinking peaks in May and June when students are celebrating proms and graduation, or not celebrating because of poor report cards and grades (www.cdc.gov/alcohol/fact-sheets/underage-drinking.htm, Fact Sheets—Underage Drinking).

- Since 1990, the number of new recreational prescription narcotic users has increased dramatically from approximately 570,000 to 2.5 million in 2000. That is a four-fold increase in only ten years. Past year and lifetime use rates of prescription drugs have surpassed most other illicit substances, aside from marijuana, in most age groups (National Drug Threat Assessment 2011, www.justice.gov/archive/ndic/topics/ndtas.htm).

- According to the partnership at DrugFree.org, more children misuse prescription painkillers every year than use cocaine. The cocaine epidemic 1989–1993 doubled drug deaths to almost 3 in 100,000. Today, the prescription drug epidemic is three times deadlier than that resulting in over 10 deaths per 100,000 in 2009.

- According to Child Trends Adolescent Health Highlight, September 2013, half of adolescents have used an illicit drug by the 12th grade.

The most common illicit drug is marijuana; about one in seven adolescents in 8th, 10th, and 12th grades combined reports having used
it in the past thirty days. About one in five 12th graders reports having
used a prescription drug without medical supervision at some time
during his or her life. About one in nine adolescents in 8th, 10th, and
12th grades combined reports having inhaled household substances
(such as glues or solvents) to get "high."

Drug Abuse: What Schools Need to Look for

Over twenty-three million Americans are addicted to alcohol and other
drugs according to Pamela Egan, Nurse Practitioner, Educator and Health
Columnist. A conservative estimate is that one in six children in school today
has a parent dependent on or addicted to alcohol or other drugs. This places
these students at high risk for social and emotional problems, as well as for
school failure, drug use, and delinquency. Most are not identified as being
"at-risk" and therefore do not receive assistance. Most adults under the influence of alcohol or other drugs are unable to provide a stable home environment. Emotional mistreatment, physical violence, and a lack of cohesiveness
often characterize these families. Silence regarding the "family secret" is
instilled in the children. Some children work hard to maintain the family's
appearance of being healthy. These students can be model students. Others
may withdraw and be invisible in a classroom of active students.

Through careful observing and listening, school personnel can identify children who need assistance. Watching how children interact with
peers, paying close attention to their drawing, and being aware of the following behavioral indicators can help educators in recognizing these students. Caution should be used by the observer while gathering as much
information as possible before seeking help for a child.

What Educators Need to Look for

A child in a drug-abusing home may:

- appear unkempt or dress inappropriately
- be tardy or absent frequently

- complain of symptoms like stomach aches or headaches

- exhibit inconsistent academic work

- seem unusually sad, hopeless, indifferent, and/or withdrawn

- be the "class clown"

- have emotional tirades or other disruptive behaviors

- seem uncomfortable during a discussion on alcohol or other drugs

- have a parent who is difficult to contact or fails to keep scheduled conferences

- have a parent who seems indifferent toward the child[1]

- be teased by peers who know of a parent's drug use

- have a parent who is observed at school or in the community under the influence of alcohol or another drug[1]

What Can School Counselors Do to Help Children Whose Parents Abuse Drugs?

When educators discuss drug or alcohol abuse it is generally in reference to student activity. Rarely, if ever, does it refer to parent abuse. Yet we are aware that parent abuse of drugs has a dramatic impact on student behavior and achievement.

1   Lead a classroom discussion on drug use and its effects on families to help normalize some of the children's feelings and encourage them to share their concerns. Provide classroom guidance lessons on other topics such as individual problem solving, resiliency, self-control, and life skills.

2   Set up small support groups. The friendships that develop in these counseling groups and the knowledge that others live in a similar environment can provide hope that students can succeed in spite of their family situation.

1 Excerpt from "An Educator's Guide to Children Affected by Parental Drug Abuse" by Leah Davis (kellybear.com/teachertips.html). Adapted by Franklin P. Schargel, used with permission.

- Furnish a compassionate, trusting, and safe place where students learn about alcohol and drug addiction.

- Provide outlets for students to explore and openly express anger, fear, or pain.

- Use a variety of methods such as discussion, games, activities, dramatic play, role-play, and art to reduce feelings of isolation, guilt, or worthlessness.

- Increase the student's protective factors such as enhancing their communication skills, building on their strengths, learning positive coping skills, and developing a feeling of self-worth and autonomy.

3   Teach the children that:

- It is not their fault that their parent(s) abuses drugs.

- There is nothing they can do to make the parent stop using drugs.

- There are individuals who care about them and who can offer help.

- There are things they can do to take care of themselves.

4   As age and grade appropriate, take these practical steps:

- Help the children plan where and when they will do their homework.

- Have them make a list of phone numbers of a relative, neighbor, or other adult that they can call on, if necessary.

- If needed, provide support in the form of furnishing school supplies, teaching a child how to use an alarm clock, providing a warm coat, and so forth.

5   Increase knowledge and awareness among school personnel of the behavioral indicators and discuss ways to help these students.

6   Start a tutoring program that uses empathetic older student or adults who would serve as positive role models and, if needed, strengthen academic skills.

7   Serve as a referral source for students and families in need of help. Your resources might include a community mental health center, Alcoholics Anonymous, Al-Anon, Alateen, alcohol/drug treatment programs, family support groups, or other services available in your area.[2]

2   Excerpt from "An Educator's Guide to Children Affected by Parental Drug Abuse" by Leah Davis (kellybear.com/teachertips.html). Adapted by Franklin P. Schargel, used with permission.

Box 4.2 *Preventing Children from Smoking*

From the Centers for Disease Control and Prevention

"Tobacco is the leading cause of preventable and premature death, killing an estimated 443,000 Americans each year. Cigarette smoking costs the nation $96 billion in direct medical costs and $97 billion in lost productivity annually. In addition to the billions in medical costs and lost productivity, tobacco is enacting a heavy toll on young people. Each day in the United States, over 3,800 young people under 18 years of age smoke their first cigarette, and over 1,000 youth under age 18 become daily cigarette smokers. The vast majority of Americans who begin daily smoking during adolescence are addicted to nicotine by young adulthood. Despite the well-known health risks, youth and adult smoking rates that had been dropping for many years have stalled." By Kathleen Sebelius, Secretary of Health and Human Services from the Executive Summary.

To be most effective, school-based programs must target young persons before they initiate tobacco use or drop out of school. Because considerable numbers of students begin using tobacco at or after age 15, tobacco-prevention education must be continued throughout high school. School-based programs should be designed to help persons avoid the difficulties of trying to stop before they are addicted to nicotine.

In this report, the term "tobacco use" refers to the use of any nicotine-containing tobacco product, such as cigarettes, electronic cigarettes ("e-cigarettes"), cigars, and smokeless tobacco. These products often contain additional substances that cause cancer in animals and humans.

RECOMMENDATIONS FOR SCHOOL HEALTH PROGRAMS TO PREVENT TOBACCO USE AND ADDICTION

The seven recommendations below summarize strategies that are effective in preventing tobacco use among youth. To ensure the greatest impact, schools should implement all seven recommendations.

According to the National Association of State Boards of Education, www.nasbe.org/healthy_schools/hs/bytopics.php?topicid=3150&cat Expand=acdnbtm_catC, each state has its own regulations about smoking on school premises.

1   **Develop and enforce a school policy on tobacco use.** The school policy on tobacco use must be consistent with state and local laws. A number of cities (i.e., New York) have banned smoking in most public places. According to www.democratandchronicle. com/.../Smoking-New-York-college-ca, sixty-seven colleges in NY are smoke or cigarette free. The *Westerly Sun* reports that smoking has been banned from Westerly High School in Rhode Island. (www.thewesterlysun.com/barker/new-smoking-policy-for-westerly-high-school-campus/article_60023bfa-8fb8-11e1-8de5-0019bb2963f4.html). This law passed by the "Smoking Restrictions in School Act"(RI General Laws Chapter 23.20-9) prohibits anyone on school grounds or 25 feet of any school buildings from using tobacco. To ensure broad support for school policies on tobacco use, representatives of relevant groups, such as students, parents, school staff and their unions, and school board members, should participate in developing and implementing the policy. Schools need to develop a tobacco-free school environment for students, staff, the school, and the district. The benefits include decreased fires and discipline problems related to student smoking, improved compliance with local and state smoking ordinances, and easier upkeep and maintenance of school facilities and grounds.

2   **Provide instruction about the short- and long-term negative physiologic and social consequences of tobacco use, social influences on tobacco use, peer norms regarding tobacco use, and refusal skills.** Programs should help students understand that tobacco use can result in decreased stamina, stained teeth, foul-smelling breath and clothes, exacerbation of asthma, and ostracism by non-smoking peers.

3   **Provide tobacco-use prevention education in kindergarten through 12th grade.** This instruction should be especially intensive in junior high or middle school and should be reinforced in high school. Programs should help students understand that some adolescents smoke because they believe it will help them be accepted by peers, appear mature, or cope with stress. Programs should help students develop other more positive means to attain such goals. Because tobacco use often begins in grades 6 through 8, more intensive instructional programs should be provided for these grade levels (4–5). Particularly important is the

year of entry into junior high or middle school when new students are exposed to older students who use tobacco at higher rates.

4   Provide program-specific training for teachers.

5   Involve parents or families in support of school-based programs to prevent tobacco use. Parents or families can play an important role in providing social and environmental support for non-smoking. Schools can capitalize on this influence by involving parents or families in program planning, in soliciting community support for programs, and in reinforcing educational messages at home. Homework assignments involving parents or families increase the likelihood that smoking is discussed at home and motivate adult smokers to consider cessation.

6   Support cessation efforts among students and all school staff who use tobacco. Schools must support student efforts to quit using tobacco, especially when tobacco use is disallowed by school policy. Cessation programs may already be available in the community through the local health department or voluntary health agency (e.g., American Cancer Society, American Heart Association, American Lung Association). Schools should identify available resources in the community and provide referral and follow-up services to students. If cessation programs for youth are not available, such programs might be jointly sponsored by the school and the local health department, voluntary health agency, other community health providers, or interested organizations (e.g., churches). For all school staff, cessation programs might help reduce burnout, lower staff absenteeism, decrease health insurance premiums, and increase commitment to overall school health goals.

7   Assess the effectiveness of tobacco-use prevention program at regular intervals.

Instructional Concepts (K–12)

Early Elementary School (K–3)

KNOWLEDGE: Students will learn that:

✓   A drug is a chemical that changes how the body works.

✓   All forms of tobacco contain a drug called nicotine.

✓ Tobacco use includes cigarettes, electronic cigarettes, and smoke-less tobacco.

✓ Tobacco use is harmful to health. Stopping tobacco use has short-term and long-term benefits.

✓ Many people who use tobacco have trouble stopping.

✓ Tobacco smoke in the air is dangerous to anyone who breathes it.

✓ People who smoke cause many fires.

✓ Some advertisements try to persuade people to use tobacco.

✓ Most young people and adults do not use tobacco.

✓ People who choose to use tobacco are not bad people.

✓ Second-hand smoke is also harmful.

ATTITUDES: Students will demonstrate:

✓ A personal commitment not to use tobacco.

✓ Pride about choosing not to use tobacco.

SKILLS: Students will be able to:

✓ Communicate knowledge and personal attitudes about tobacco use.

✓ Encourage other people not to use tobacco.

Later Elementary School (4–6)

KNOWLEDGE: Students will learn that:

✓ Stopping tobacco use has short- and long-term benefits.*

✓ Environmental tobacco smoke is dangerous to health.*

✓ Most young people and adults do not use tobacco.*

✓ Nicotine, contained in all forms of tobacco, is an addictive drug.

✓ Tobacco use has short-term and long-term physiologic and cosmetic consequences.

✓ Personal feelings, family, peers, and the media influence decisions about tobacco use.

✓   Tobacco advertising is often directed toward young people.

✓   Young people can resist pressure to use tobacco.

✓   Laws, rules, and policies regulate the sale and use of tobacco.

ATTITUDES: Students will demonstrate:

✓   A personal commitment not to use tobacco.*

✓   Pride about choosing not to use tobacco.*

✓   Support for others' decisions not to use tobacco.

✓   Responsibility for personal health.

SKILLS: Students will be able to:

✓   Communicate knowledge and personal attitudes about tobacco use.*

✓   Encourage other people not to use tobacco.*

✓   Demonstrate skills to resist tobacco use.

✓   State the benefits of a smoke-free environment.

✓   Develop counterarguments to tobacco advertisements and other promotional materials.

✓   Support people who are trying to stop using tobacco.

Middle School/Junior High School

KNOWLEDGE: Students will learn that:

✓   Most young people and adults do not use tobacco.*

✓   Tobacco use has short-term and long-term physiologic, cosmetic, social, and economic consequences.*

✓   Tobacco manufacturers use various strategies to direct advertisements to young people.*

✓   Young people can resist pressure to use tobacco.*

✓   Laws, rules, and policies regulate the sale and use of tobacco.*

✓   Cigarette smoking and smokeless tobacco use have direct health consequences.

✓   Maintaining a tobacco-free environment has health benefits.

✓   Tobacco use is an unhealthy way to manage weight and stress.

✓ Community organizations have information about tobacco use and can help people stop using tobacco.

✓ Smoking cessation programs can be successful.

✓ Tobacco contains other harmful substances in addition to nicotine.

ATTITUDES: Students will demonstrate:

✓ A personal commitment not to use tobacco.*

✓ Pride about choosing not to use tobacco.*

✓ Support for others' decisions not to use tobacco.*

✓ Responsibility for personal health.*

✓ Confidence in personal ability to resist tobacco use.

SKILLS: Students will be able to:

✓ Communicate knowledge and personal attitudes about tobacco use.*

✓ Encourage other people not to use tobacco.*

✓ Demonstrate skills to resist tobacco use.*

✓ State the benefits of a smoke-free environment.*

✓ Develop counterarguments to tobacco advertisements and other promotional materials.*

✓ Support people who are trying to stop using tobacco.*

✓ Identify and counter strategies used in tobacco advertisements and other promotional materials.

✓ Develop methods for coping with tobacco use by parents and with other difficult personal situations, such as peer pressure to use tobacco.

✓ Request a smoke-free environment.

Senior High School

KNOWLEDGE: Students will learn that:

✓ Most young people and adults do not smoke.*

✓ Tobacco use has short-term and long-term physiologic, cosmetic, social, and economic consequences.*

✓ Tobacco manufacturers use various strategies to direct advertisements to young people.*

✓ Young people can resist pressure to use tobacco.*

✓ Cigarette smoking and smokeless tobacco use have direct health consequences.*

✓ Tobacco use is an unhealthy way to manage weight and stress.*

✓ Community organizations have information about tobacco use and can help people stop using tobacco.*

✓ Smoking cessation programs can be successful.*

✓ Tobacco use during pregnancy has harmful effects on the fetus.

✓ Schools and community organizations can promote a smoke-free environment.

✓ Many people find it hard to stop using tobacco, despite knowledge about the health hazards of tobacco use.

ATTITUDES: Students will demonstrate:

✓ A personal commitment not to use tobacco.*

✓ Pride about choosing not to use tobacco.*

✓ Support for others' decisions not to use tobacco.*

✓ Responsibility for personal health.*

✓ Confidence in personal ability to resist tobacco use.*

✓ Willingness to use school and community resources for information about, and help with, resisting or quitting tobacco use.

SKILLS: Students will be able to:

✓ Communicate knowledge and personal attitudes about tobacco use.*

✓ Encourage other people not to use tobacco.*

✓ Demonstrate skills to resist tobacco use.*

✓ State the benefits of a smoke-free environment.*

✓ Develop counterarguments to tobacco advertisements and other promotional materials.*

✓ Support people who are trying to stop using tobacco.*

✓ Identify and counter strategies used in tobacco advertisements and other promotional materials.*

✓ Develop methods for coping with tobacco use by parents and with other difficult personal situations, such as peer pressure to use tobacco.*

✓ Use school and community resources for information about and help with, resisting or quitting tobacco use.

✓ Initiate school and community action to support a smoke-free environment.

* These concepts reinforce content introduced during earlier grades.

(Source: 2012 Surgeon General's Report—Preventing Tobacco Use Among Youth and Young Adults, www.cdc.gov/tobacco/data_statistics/sgr/2012/index.htm)

Recognizing Signs and Symptoms of Drug Abuse and Drug Addiction

Different drugs have different physical effects and therefore it is difficult to distinguish the symptoms of addiction. In addition, drug abusers often try to conceal their symptoms and downplay their problem. Drug use among teens and tweens is growing in America. It is important to recognize that teens and children respond differently to drugs. You cannot treat drug abuse in children the same way you do in adults. Certainly there are similarities, but there are also important differences that demand a different approach when dealing with teens and tweens. Here are a few warning signs:

Physical Warning Signs of Drug Abuse

- Bloodshot eyes, pupils larger or smaller than usual.
- Sudden weight loss or weight gain.
- Deterioration of physical appearance, personal grooming habits.
- Unusual smells on breath, body, or clothing.
- Tremors, slurred speech, or impaired coordination.

Behavioral Signs of Drug Abuse

- Drop in attendance and performance at work or school.
- Engaging in secretive or suspicious behaviors.
- Sudden change in friends, favorite hangouts, and hobbies.
- Frequently getting into trouble (fights, accidents, illegal activities).

Psychological Warning Signs of Drug Abuse

- Unexplained change in personality or attitude.
- Sudden mood swings, irritability, or angry outbursts.
- Periods of unusual hyperactivity, agitation, or giddiness.
- Lack of motivation; appears lethargic or "spaced out."
- Appears fearful, anxious, or paranoid, with no reason.

Warning Signs of Commonly Abused Drugs

- **Marijuana.** Glassy, red eyes; loud talking, inappropriate laughter followed by sleepiness; loss of interest, motivation; weight gain or loss.
- **Depressants (including Xanax, Valium, GHB).** Contracted pupils; drunklike; difficulty concentrating; clumsiness; poor judgment; slurred speech; sleepiness.
- **Stimulants (including amphetamines, cocaine, crystal meth).** Dilated pupils; hyperactivity; euphoria; irritability; anxiety; excessive talking followed by depression or excessive sleeping at odd times; weight loss; dry mouth and nose.
- **Inhalants (glues, aerosols, vapors).** Watery eyes; impaired vision, memory and thought; secretions from the nose or rashes around the nose and mouth; headaches and nausea; appearance of intoxication; drowsiness; poor muscle control; changes in appetite; anxiety; irritability.
- **Hallucinogens (LSD, PCP).** Dilated pupils; bizarre and irrational behavior including paranoia, aggression, hallucinations; mood swings;

detachment from people; absorption with self or other objects; slurred speech; confusion.

- **Heroin.** Contracted pupils; no response of pupils to light; needle marks; sleeping at unusual times; sweating; vomiting; coughing, sniffling; twitching; loss of appetite.

How do you recognize drug use, abuse, or addiction in teens? Many teens will exhibit the same signs as adults. However, their age, lack of mobility and resources present some different behaviors to watch for. Any of these behaviors could indicate that your tween or teen has a drug problem:

- **School attendance.** If your child exhibits a sudden, active dislike for school or looks for excuses for staying at home or feigns illness, contact the school. See if your child's attendance records match with your knowledge. Playing hooky or cutting class can be a sign of drug use.

- **School performance.** A drop in performance, failing courses, or minimally passing grades can indicate drug use.

- **Lack of interest.** Lack of interest in extracurricular activities—dropping out of clubs or band or sports—can indicate drug use. If your teen stops doing things that used to give him/her pleasure, find out why. Drugs could be involved.

- **Poor health.** Repeated incidents of listlessness, apathy, or depression can indicate drug use. Drug use can lower the immune system, making your child more susceptible to colds and disease.

- **Change in appearance.** Teens are obsessed about their appearance. Any sudden lack of attention to clothing, grooming, or physical appearance is a warning sign of possible drug use.

- **Behavior change.** Any sudden or significant change in your child's behavior is a warning sign. While it may not always signal drug use, behavior changes indicate a problem. If the issue is not addressed, the teen may resort to drugs as a way to escape his/her problems. Watch for any changes in relationships with family members and friends.

- **Excessive privacy.** Teens like their privacy, but secretive behavior, always locked doors, or excessive time spent in their rooms can be signs of drug use. If your teen would rather stay home in his/her room than go out with friends, he could be using drugs.

● **New friends.** If your child stops seeing old, established friends and starts hanging out with new friends, drugs could be involved. Drug users prefer to hang out with other drug users. Listen to your conscience. If you think your teen is hanging out with "bad" friends or the "wrong crowd," you should investigate. But it's important to remember that even "clean-cut," "good" kids can be drug users and providers.

● **Money.** Sudden or repeated requests for money can signal drug use. If you notice money disappearing from your wallet or purse, even if it's just small amounts, you teen may be stealing to finance his/her habit. Check the pizza stash in the kitchen cupboard and any other places you hide money. Likewise, if things start to disappear from your house, your teen may be selling, pawning, or trading them for drugs.

5 Internet Safety

Young people are using modern technology, including cell phones, computers, tablets, and the Internet to communicate with others in the United States and throughout the world. This modern form of communications has allowed young people to more easily develop relationships; some with people they have never met in person.

This technology has many potential benefits for them. It allows young people to communicate with friends and family on a regular basis. It also provides opportunities to make positive social connections for those teenagers and pre-teens that have difficulty developing friendships in traditional social settings. In addition, regular Internet access allows them to quickly increase their knowledge on a wide variety of topics.

However, these tools do not come without possible risks. Technology can offer instant information—and misinformation. Some people can use electronic media to embarrass, harass, or threaten their peers. Increasing numbers of teens are becoming victims of this new form of violence. This harassment is described using a variety of terms including cyberbullying, Internet harassment, and Internet bullying. It can cause emotional distress and lead to problems at school.

Children consider the Internet to be their friend. They place all sorts of things on Myspace and Facebook. They spend large amounts of time texting, instant messaging, or sending pictures from their smart phones. They do not believe they should have any limits imposed on their Internet access. But it is part of the responsibility of educators to insure a child's safety in the virtual world.

Background

Electronics are ever-present in young people's lives. Adults used to be concerned about the number of hours of television that young people watched. Now they are concerned with how much time they spend on the computer, playing video games, and on the Internet.

- While access to computers and the Internet varies by parental income, education, and ethnicity, overall, 88.9 percent of all households owned a personal computer, and 81.4 percent of all households had Internet access. Among households with Internet access, 48.3 percent had high-speed Internet at home. However, the impact of this difference was lessened by the fact that over 60 percent of families with annual household income of $10,000–$25,000, and nearly 70 percent of families with only a high school education had Internet access at home (A.E. Carroll, F.P. Rivara, B. Ebel, F.J. Zimmerman, and D.A. Christakis, 'Household computer and Internet access: The digital divide in a pediatric clinic population', www.ncbi.nlm.nih.gov/pmc/articles/PMC1560660/).

- According to the University of Michigan study, 76 percent of US children have computers and access to the Internet in their homes, and those between 12 and 17 years of age log in approximately five hours a week to use them (www.ur.umich.edu/0405/Dec06_04/20. shtml). Comparatively, they spend up to 14 hours a week watching television. There's mounting evidence that this "sit time" is a major contributor to the obesity epidemic (www.hsph.harvard.edu/obesity-prevention-source/obesity-causes/television-and-sedentary-behavior-and-obesity/). As children sit in front of televisions and computers, they do not participate in outdoor sports and activities.

- The New York Times cites a study which found that half of American children have a television in their bedroom (www.nytimes.com/ 2008/03/04/health/04well.html); one study of 3rd graders put the number at 70 percent. The Kaiser Family Foundation released a study in 2008 indicating that 31 percent of kids aged 8 to 18 have a computer in the bedroom, and 20 percent have Internet access. And one in four high-school-aged children uses instant message software in the bedroom. If parents do not monitor their child's use of the Internet or of watching television, they do not know what time their children go to sleep or what they are doing. This may account for the students scoring lower on tests, being sleepy, or being more able to be bullied.

- Nearly six out of ten US parents of children aged 8 to12 have provided those children with cell phones (www.consumerreports.org/cro/news/2012/07/most-kids-8-to-12-now-have-cell-phones-should-yours/index.htm). According to a study done by Pew Internet and America Life Project, more than 75 percent of 2010 teens have a cell phone. About 88 percent of all teen cell phone users are texters. More than half of teen texters report texting on a daily basis. In fact, one in three teens report sending more than a hundred messages per day (that's about 3,000 texts a month). About 15 percent of teen texters report sending more than two hundred texts a day or 6,000 texts a month! Some of these teens admitted to sleeping with their phone under their pillow so it will vibrate at night when they get a text (February 3, 2010, http://pewinternet.org/Reports/2010/Teens-and-Mobile-Phones.aspx).

The study *Zero to Six: Electronic Media in the Lives of Infants, Toddlers and Preschoolers* was conducted by the Kaiser Family Foundation and the Children's Digital Media Centers. It is the first publicly released national study of media use among the very youngest children, from 6 months to 6 years old. The report is based on a survey of more than 2,000 students in grades 3 to 12 that was conducted from October 2008 to May 2009. This report is based on the results of a nationally representative, random digit dial telephone survey of 1,065 parents of children ages 6 months to 6 years old, conducted from April 11 to June 9, 2003 (related resources will be available at kff.org/other/report/zero-to-six-electronic-media-in-the/). This study found that:

- The average young American now spends practically every waking minute—except for the time in school—using a smart phone, computer, television, or other electronic device. Those aged 8 to 18 spend more than seven and a half hours a day with such devices, compared with less than six and a half hours five years ago, when the study was last conducted. And that does not count the hour and a half that youths spend texting, or the half-hour they talk on their cell phones. And because so many of them are multitasking—say, surfing the Internet while listening to music—they pack an average of nearly 11 hours of media content into that seven and a half hours. The study found that young people's media consumption grew far more in the last five years than from 1999 to 2004, as sophisticated mobile technology like iPods and smart phones brought media access into teenagers' pockets and beds.

- While most of the young people in the study got good grades, 47 percent of the heaviest media users—those who consumed at least 16 hours a day—had mostly Cs or lower, compared with 23 percent of those who typically consumed media three hours a day or less. The heaviest media users were also more likely than the lightest users to report that they were bored or sad, or that they got into trouble, did not get along well with their parents, and were not happy at school.

- On average, young people spend about two hours a day consuming media on a mobile device, the study found. They spend almost another hour on "old" content like television or music delivered through newer pathways like the website Hulu or iTunes. Youths now spend more time listening to or watching media on their cell phones, or playing games, than talking on them.

- The study found that more than seven in ten youths have a TV in their bedroom, and about a third have a computer with Internet access in their bedroom.

- The heaviest media users, the study found, are black and Hispanic youths and "tweens," or those ages 11 to 14.

- Children 6 and under spend an average of two hours a day using screen media (1:58), about the same amount of time they spend playing outside (2:01), and well over the amount they spend reading or being read to (39 minutes). New interactive digital media have become an integral part of children's lives. Nearly half (48 percent) of children 6 and under have used a computer (31 percent of 0- to 3-year-olds and 70 percent of 4- to 6-year-olds). Just under a third (30 percent) have played video games (14 percent of 0- to 3-year-olds and 50 percent of 4- to 6-year-olds). Even the youngest children—those under 2—are widely exposed to electronic media. Forty-three percent of those under 2 watch TV every day, and 26 percent have a TV in their bedroom (the American Academy of Pediatrics "urges parents to avoid television for children under 2 years old"). In any given day, two-thirds (68 percent) of children under 2 will use screen media, for an average of just over two hours (2:05).

- A third of all 0- to 6-year-olds (36 percent) have a TV in their bedroom, more than one in four (27 percent) have a VCR or DVD, one in ten have a video game player, and 7 percent have a computer. Thirty percent of 0- to 3-year-olds have a TV in their room, and 43 percent of 4- to 6-year-olds do. When children have TVs and other media in their bedrooms, it's more difficult for parents to monitor what they're doing.

- In a typical day about one in four (27 percent) 4- to 6-year-olds uses a computer, and those who do spend an average of just over an hour at the keyboard (1:04). More than a third (39 percent) of 4- to 6-year-olds use a computer several times a week or more; 37 percent in this age group can turn the computer on by themselves, and 40 percent can load a CD-ROM.

- Many children are growing up in homes where the TV is an ever-present companion: two-thirds (65 percent) live in homes where the TV is left on at least half the time or more, even if no one is watching, and one-third (36 percent) live in homes where the TV is on "always" or "most of the time" (the latter group are considered "heavy" TV households).

- According to the study, children who have a TV in their bedroom or who live in "heavy" TV households spend significantly more time watching than other children do, and less time reading or playing outside. Those with a TV in their room spend an average of 22 minutes more a day watching TV and videos than other children do. They are also less likely to read every day (59 percent v. 68 percent), and spend less time reading when they do read (six minutes less a day). In fact, they are less likely than other children to be able to read at all (34 percent of children ages 4–6 from "heavy" TV households can read, compared to 56 percent of other children that age).

- Half (50 percent) of all 4- to 6-year-olds have played video games, and one in four (25 percent) play several times a week or more. Differences between boys and girls have already begun to emerge at this young age: 56 percent of boys have played video games, compared to 36 percent of girls; and in a typical day, 24 percent of boys will play, compared to 8 percent of girls.

- A survey by the Pew Research Center found half of all students in higher income families have access to the Internet at home through a computer or mobile device. The figure drops to 20 percent for middle-income children and just 3 percent of students from poor homes. The growing disparity of Internet access is leading to a gap in performance, about 56 percent of teachers said (source: www.livestrong.com/article/236977-how-much-time-do-children-spend-on-the-computer/#ixzz2PVgApdMj).

Should Cell Phones Be Allowed in Schools?

As the percentage of students in high school, middle school, and even elementary school who own cell phones continues to grow, the debate over whether they should be allowed to use them in school becomes more heated.

The Pros

The chief argument in favor of allowing cell phones at school is safety. Students can contact their parents or another authority figure in case of an emergency, and vice versa. Furthermore, parents can reach their children at any time and learn their whereabouts. Cell phones provide an extra measure of security, and they're convenient.

And students will use them anyway. According to MSNBC, Common Sense Media conducted a poll that revealed that 63 percent of students still use cell phones at schools even where there are cell phone bans.

In his blog post "I lost something very important to me" on "Weblogg-ed," a website dedicated to technological resources in the classroom, Will Richardson wondered about the messages cell phone bans send. He wrote, "What does [confiscating cell phones] teach those kids? First, it teaches them that they don't deserve to be empowered with technology the same way adults are. Second, that the tools that adults use all the time in their everyday lives to communicate are not relevant to their own communication needs."

The Cons

But they're distracting. Even if their phones are on silent, students can text and go online during class. Educators opposed to allowing cell phones in schools also cite cyberbullying, the use of phones and other technology to harass peers, as a reason to leave them at home.

Cell phones can also facilitate cheating. Common Sense Media found that two-thirds of students surveyed claimed that their classmates used cell phones to cheat on coursework, while one-third said they themselves had done so. Armed with high-tech phones, students can browse the Internet and ask their friends for answers to test questions, or store information to give their friends later on.

"When students have cell phones in their possession during school hours, many disciplinary problems stem from [cell phone] abuse," Jon Akers, Executive Director of the Kentucky Center for School Safety, writes in his article, "Student Cell Phones Should Be Prohibited in K–12 Schools" (the article is available for download on the Kentucky Center for School Safety website, www.kycss.org/index2.php).

He adds, "The current barrage of illegal and immoral acts committed daily (on cell phones by students during the school day) far outweigh the parent's right to talk (and in some cases, interfere) with their children during a school emergency."

For me, the real question is how do schools learn how to incorporate the use of technology instead of banning it?

Suggested Student Discipline Rules

Schools should consider submitting Student Discipline Rules to students and their parents or guardians involving the use of electronic communication devices. The rules in Figure 5.1 were developed by the Center for Education Policy and Law at the University of San Diego. It is suggested that both students and their parents sign it.

Not only should schools make rules regarding student discipline, but they also need to insure that students and parents are made aware of these rules. Below are a set of rules designed by the Center for Education Policy and Law, University of San Diego. Schools can modify or amend them to their individual cultures.

SUGGESTED STUDENT DISCIPLINE RULES (Short Version)
Student Misuse of Electronic Communication Devices
in Junior High and High Schools

Source: Center for Education Policy and Law, University of San Diego, October 2010

Dear Parents and Guardians,

We recognize that electronic communication devices are an important part of our everyday world and are increasingly being used in teaching and learning. However, we do not want these devices to interfere with the students' learning environment.

Figure 5.1 Suggested student discipline rules

(Continued)

Please read the following discipline rules with your student and return the form with your signatures. Thank you.[1]

1. Students must follow school rules when using any of the following electronic communication devices (ECDs):
    - Cell phones
    - Computers
    - Pagers
    - Portable game units
    - Other mechanisms that enable users to communicate electronically person-to-person or through Internet social networking sites such as Facebook, MySpace, and Twitter.

2. School rules apply when students are at school or attending a school-sponsored or related activity off-campus. They apply when students are:
    - Attending class
    - Socializing in hallways and elsewhere on school grounds
    - Using school media centers, restrooms, lockerrooms, gyms, and other school facilities
    - Going to and from school
    - Eating lunch on or off campus
    - Attending school-sponsored activities off campus, such as field trips, dances
    - Attending school-related activities off campus, such as football away games

3. The following will result in student discipline at any of the above activities:
    - Refusal to turn off an (Electronic Communication Device) ECD when told to by a teacher, administrator, coach, counselor, or other school official
    - Damaging an ECD owned by the school

4. - Causing disruption
    - Using an ECD to cheat, including getting and giving answers to tests and copying from the internet
    - Using an ECD to bully, threaten, harass, or attack another student or school personnel whether or not communicated directly to that person
    - Sending (or asking to receive) pictures or videos of people who are partially or completely undressed, or are pretending to or actually performing a sexual act

---

1 These rules are developed in the context of federal and California law. Whether they are appropriate for other states depends upon the law in those states. It may be appropriate to have both teachers and students review these rules to see if they are understandable or should be reworded to make them so. These rules are suggestive only and are not intended to take the place of expert advice and assistance from a lawyer. If specific legal advice or assistance is required, the services of a competent professional should be sought.

5. Additionally, the school may punish students who misuse ECDs away from school on their own time if both of the following are true:
   - The student's use of the ECD causes significant disruption at school or serious harm to the school, other students, or school personnel
   - The student knew, or should have known, that the harm would happen

6. When a student misuses an ECD, the school may do the following, as long as the severity of the school's action matches the seriousness of the student's misuse of the ECD:
   - Search the ECD within the context of the alleged misuse
   - Warn the student, verbally or in writing
   - Take away the ECD. Depending upon the offense, the school may keep the ECD for the rest of the school day or longer
   - Deny the student the privilege of participating in extracurricular and athletic activities
   - Contact the student's parents, school security, or the police
   - Suspend or expel the student from school in accord with student discipline procedures

I have received a copy of these Student Discipline Rules governing my use of electronic communication devices (ECDs). I understand that failure to follow these rules may result in discipline and affect my right to use ECDs while at school and at school-sponsored or related activities both on and off campus.

_____ Name of Student (print)

Signature Date _____

Signature of Parent/Guardian _____

Date _____

Please return this form to the school office no later than _____.

Internet Safety Guidelines for Students

Children need to be protected from online predators. Schools are in a position of providing rules for students to use. With the increased use of social networks, smart phones, and tablets, they are vulnerable to online assaults.

To students: your safety and your family's safety may depend on how you use the Internet.

- You and your family should determine who uses the computer, when you can use it, and for how long.

- Protect your passwords. Let your parent have a copy of your password list just in case you lose your list.

- But don't tell your best friend, any friend, or anyone you met online.

- Passwords are a secret between you, your parents, and the websites where you use them.

- When you select your password, be sure that the letters and numbers do not make any sense. Do not use your birthday, your address, or anything else that might give a clue to who you are and ensure that you have a different password for each website.

- Don't use for a password words that tell something about you, like your nickname, your favorite color, your pet's name, or a word that describes you in some way.

- Make your passwords difficult for someone who knows you to figure out (example: x8h4p2).

- Do not open any email attachments unless you confirm with the sender they actually sent the attachment. Print the list of infectious email attachments and subjects and keep it available by your computer.

- If you are old enough that your parents allow you in chat rooms, remember that even though persons are acting your age in the safe chat room, they could be a bad person.

- Don't arrange or agree to meet, face-to-face or in phone conversation, with another computer user without your parent's knowledge even if they say they are in serious trouble and need your help right now.

- Watch younger brothers or sisters when they are connected to the Internet. Be sure they are not talking to strangers or visiting a "bad" website.

- Tell your parents when anyone uses bad language or writes things that make you uncomfortable.

- Don't answer email from a stranger.

- Tell your parents when someone asks you to keep their emails, conversations, or friendship a secret.

- Never send to any person or post at any website pictures or files without your parent's knowledge.

- If someone sends you an inappropriate message picture or says anything that makes you uncomfortable, tell your parent or another adult that you trust.

- Do not indicate your name, gender, age, or race to anyone or on any website, or social network.

(Source: FBI, www.fbi.gov/fun-games/kids/kids-safety)

What Parents Can Do to Protect Their Child from the Internet

Children enjoy the interactivity of computers and smart telephones but they also need to be made aware of the dangers.

- **Giving away personal information.** Insist that your children never reveal their names, addresses, telephone numbers, their ages, or the schools they attend. If your child has an email address, check it to make sure it doesn't have clues to their identity such as first or last name, or their birth date.

- **"Free" gifts.** Children like to believe that every time they enter a contest, they will win. Spammers are aware of this naiveté and take advantage of it by offering "free gifts" in exchange for information. Train your child not to complete online surveys or to buy anything without seeking your permission.

- **Don't be too trusting.** Children who use social media sites like Twitter or Facebook do not realize that some people using the sites may be disguising themselves and their identities. Your children should never agree to meet with anyone they do not know whom they met online.

- **Online means forever.** Children tend to post suggestive pictures or personal information on the web. Colleges and potential employers are accessing that information. Teach your children never to post things on the web that they would later in life regret.

6 Violent School Incidents

Every time there is a highly publicized violent school incident, there is the widespread perception that school violence is rampant in the United States. For example, after the 1999 Columbine shooting, a Gallup poll found that two-thirds of Americans believed that a similar incident could happen in their community. As a result, many school districts instituted zero-tolerance policies where students were expelled for seemingly minor offenses like bringing a plastic knife to school or pointing a finger like a gun, or shooting a paper clip with a rubber band.

After the high-profile shootings in 2012–2013, there were renewed recommendations to arm teachers with guns and even a call to issue Kevlar-coated textbooks to students to use as bullet shields (R. Borum, D.G. Cornell, W. Modzeleski, and S.R. Jimerson, "What Can Be Done about School Shootings? A Review of The Evidence," *Educational Researcher* 39(1): 27–37). Schools across the country have installed metal detectors similar to those used in airports. Rather than rely on unrealistic measures, it may be more useful for schools to consider less dramatic but more practical *prevention* approaches. Strategies to maintain school safety should be based on a factual assessment of the risk of violent crime, and on evidence of what prevention methods are really effective.

In an effort to protect students and staff, schools tend to overreact, creating draconian and punitive rules that far exceed juvenile pranks like flying paper airplanes, throwing "spitballs," shooting a paper clip with a rubber band, or pointing a finger like a gun. As a result of these zero-tolerance policies, which have greatly expanded nationwide, students are sometimes suspended or expelled for minor offenses like those listed. Research indicates that zero-tolerance rules do not have an effect on student behavior (*Are Zero Tolerance Policies Effective in the Schools? An Evidentiary Review and Recommendations,* December 2008, American Psychological Association Zero Tolerance Task Force, www.apa.org/pubs/info/reports/zero-tolerance.pdf).

Background: Dealing with Gun Violence

While the number of shootings has decreased and the number of students injured has decreased, each event has caused consternation from the media, the public, and parents. Violent crime in schools has decreased significantly since the early 1990s. Research by Cornell University and others state that rates of school violence are going steadily down, but it's clear that schools are the safest place for a student to be. Violence in North American schools is an unfortunate reality for today's children. Stricter discipline at school, increased parental involvement, and stricter gun control are some of the ways that Americans and Canadians alike believe these tragedies can be averted.

- Thanks to the exposure in the media, Americans are increasingly concerned about violence-free schools. They now view gun control as an important factor in the cause and prevention of school shootings.

- Just under half of Americans (46 percent) reported in 2001 that the availability and ease of obtaining guns by students is an extremely important cause of school shootings, which placed it second on a list of eight causes behind family home life.

- Since the Sandy Hook, Newtown, Connecticut shootings, US parents of school-aged children are more concerned about their children's safety at school than they were before the event, with the percentage saying they fear for their oldest child's safety rising eight percentage points to 33 percent. This is the highest level recorded since October 2006 when 35 percent were fearful (source: www.gallup.com/poll/159584/parents-fear-children-safety-school-rises-slightly.aspx, December 28, 2012).

- A poll conducted by CBS News (www.cbsnews.com/8301-250_162-57559669/poll-support-for-stricter-gun-control-at-10-year-high/) indicates that 57 percent of Americans now say gun control laws should be made more strict. There has even been a call for the arming of educators in schools. An Arkansas school district has been arming more than twenty teachers and staff, www.foxnews.com/us/2013/07/30/arkansas-school-district-arming-more-than-20-teachers-staff/?test=latestnews#ixzz2adrhND00.

- Nearly one-third of all parents say they fear for the safety of their child when he or she is at school. In fact, the percentage of parents saying they fear for their oldest child's physical safety at school has remained similar to what it was in an August 2001 poll (32 percent in August 2001 and 31 percent in August 2002).

- Parents of children in public school are nearly twice as likely to say they worry as those with children in non-public schools—32 percent versus 18 percent.

- Concern about school safety takes a big leap among all parents when children move from elementary school to middle school and high school. Just 24 percent of parents whose oldest child is in elementary school express concern for their child's safety at school, but 47 percent of parents whose oldest child is in middle school or high school do.

- According to the National Youth Violence Prevention Resource Center "Facts For Teens," "In recent years, fewer teens are carrying weapons, teen murder arrests have dropped by almost 60%, and the arrest rate for violent crimes is down 36% from its peak in 1994" (www.herkimer county.org/content/Departments/View/11:field=services;/content/DepartmentServices/View/68:field=documents;/content/Documents/File/122.pdf).

- Gang violence has been proliferating since 1980, when there were about 2,000 gangs in 266 cities. By 1996, according to the Office of Juvenile Justice's *Promising Strategies to Reduce Gun Violence,* (www.ojjdp.gov/pubs/gun_violence/173950.pdf), there were 31,000 gangs with 846,000 members in 4,800 cities and towns. The risk of being killed is sixty times greater among young gang members than in the general population, and in some cities, far higher. For example, the St. Louis youth gang homicide rate is 1,000 times higher than the US homicide rate. Gang membership also appears to increase individual participation in drug use, gun-carrying violence, and involvement in drug sales.

Gangs reportedly operate in 41 percent of urban schools, 26 percent of suburban schools, and 20 percent of rural schools.

Strategies for Preventing School Violence

(Adapted from *Dropout Prevention Fieldbook* © 2003 by Franklin P. Schargel.)

- Shift culture to cooperative thinking about techniques that foster conflict resolution.
- Meet the basic needs of students through support agencies.
- Provide a school resource office from the local police force.
- Initiate a no-bullying program.
- Provide peer mediation.
- Implement a conflict resolution curriculum.
- Teach anger management techniques.
- Actively engage all constituencies (law enforcement officials, parents, the business community, Chamber of Commerce).
- Eliminate or control gangs.
- Have a crisis management plan developed with input of students, parents, police, and the outside community.
- Be aware of what is happening on campus, with cliques, gangs.
- Be proactive without being repressive.
- Don't overreact.
- Train staff to address practical steps to prevent school violence.
- Involve disenfranchised. Provide a voice for everyone.
- Accept "zero tolerance" for threats and violence.
- Develop *and deploy* a School Security Plan.
- Establish fair, equitable rules, and consequences and *enforce them.*
- Be aware that no matter what you do, things will happen.

What Can Be Done to Prevent School Violence

(Adapted from *Preventing Bullying: A Manual For Schools and Communities,* US Department of Education.)

Every day in our nation's schools, children are threatened, teased, taunted, and tormented by other students. For some children, school violence is a fact of life that they are told to accept as a part of growing up. Those who fail to recognize and stop school violence as it occurs actually promote violence, sending the message to children that might indeed makes right.

The application of a comprehensive model includes the following core elements.

School-Level Interventions

- Administration of a student questionnaire to determine the nature and extent of violence at the school.

- Teacher in-service days to review finding from the questionnaire, discuss problems of violence, and plan the school's violence prevention efforts.

- Schoolwide events to launch the program (e.g., via school public address or assemblies).

- Increased supervision in areas that are hot spots for violence at the school.

- Development of schoolwide rules and sanctions against any form of violence.

- Parent involvement in school activities (e.g., highlighting the program at PTA meetings, school open houses, and special violence prevention programs; encouraging parents' participation in planning activities and acting as chaperones at school events).

Individual Interventions

- Immediate intervention by school staff in all violence incidents.

- Involvement of parents of perpetrators of violence and victims, where appropriate.

- Formation of "friendship groups" or other supports for students who are victims of violence.

- Involvement of school counselors or mental health professionals, where appropriate.

Community Activities

- Efforts to make the program known among a wide range of residents in the local community (e.g., convening meetings with leaders of the community to discuss the school's program and problems associated with bullying and other forms of violence, encouraging local media coverage of the school's efforts, engaging students in efforts to discuss their school's program with informal leaders of the community).

- Involvement of community members in the school's anti-violence activities (e.g., soliciting assistance from local business to support aspects of the program, involving community members in school-district-wide "Violence-Free Day" events).

Before implementing any efforts to address violence at school, school administrators should keep in mind that:

- Ideally, efforts should begin early—as children transition into kinder-garten—and continue throughout a child's formal education.

- Effective programs require strong leadership and ongoing commit-ment on the part of school personnel.

- Ongoing staff development and training are important to sustain programs.

- Parental and community involvement in the planning and execution of such programs is critical.

Following are suggested action steps, strategies, and resources that school administrators, educators, students, and parents can employ in an effort to stopping violence in schools.

Action Steps for School Administrators

- Assess the awareness and the scope of the violence problems at your school through student and staff surveys.

- Closely supervise children on the playground and in classrooms, hall-ways, restrooms, cafeterias, study halls, and other areas where bully-ing and violence occur in your school.

- Conduct schoolwide assemblies and teacher/staff in-service training to raise awareness regarding the problems of bullying and violence.

- Post and publicize clear behavior standards, including rules against violence for all students. Consistently and fairly enforce such standards.

- Encourage parent participation by establishing on-campus parents' centers that recruit, coordinate, and encourage parents to take part in the educational process and in volunteering to assist in school activities and projects.

- Establish a confidential reporting system that allows children to report victimization and that records the details of violent incidents.

- Ensure that your school has met all legally required policies and grievance procedures for sexual discrimination. Make these procedures known to parents and students.

- Receive and listen receptively to parents who report violence. Establish procedures whereby such reports are investigated and resolved expeditiously to avoid perpetuating violence.

- Develop strategies to reward student for positive behavioral acts.

- Provide schoolwide and classroom activities that are designed to build self-esteem by spotlighting special talents, hobbies, interests, and abilities of all students and that foster mutual understanding of and appreciation for differences in others.

Strategies for Classroom Teachers

- Provide students with opportunities to talk about bullying and other forms of violence and enlist their support in defining unacceptable forms of behavior.

- Involve students in establishing classroom rules against bullying. Such rules may include a commitment from the teacher to not "look the other way" when incidents involving bullying occur.

- Provide classroom activities and discussions related to bullying and violence, including the harm that they cause and strategies to reduce them.

- Develop a classroom action plan to ensure that students know what to do when they observe a violent incident.

- Teach cooperation by assigning projects that require collaboration. Such cooperation teaches students how to compromise and how to assert without demanding. Take care to vary grouping of participants and to monitor the treatment of participants in each group.

- Take immediate action when violence is observed. All teachers and school staff must let children know that they care and will not allow anyone to be mistreated. By taking immediate action and dealing directly with the perpetrator, adults support both the victim and the witnesses.

- Confront bullies and the person responsible for the violent actions in private. Challenging a bully in front of his/her peers may actually enhance his/her status and lead to further aggression.

- Notify the parents of both victims and those accused of violence when a confrontation occurs, and seek to resolve the problem expeditiously at school.

- Refer both victim and aggressors to counseling whenever appropriate.

- Provide protection for victims whenever necessary. Such protection may include creating a buddy system whereby students have a particular friend or older buddy on whom they can depend and with whom they share class schedule information and plans for the school day.

- Listen receptively to parents who report violence and investigate reported circumstances so that immediate and appropriate school action may be taken.

- Avoid attempts to mediate a bullying situation. The difference in power between victims and bullies may cause victims to feel further victimized by the process or believe that they are somehow at fault.

Strategies for Students

Students may not know what to do when they observe a violent act. Classroom discussions and activities may help students develop a variety of appropriate actions that they can take when they witness or experience such victimization. For instance, depending on the situation and their own level of comfort, students can:

- seek immediate help from an adult;

- report victimization incidents to school personnel;

- speak up and/or offer support to the victim when they see him/her being bullied or assaulted—for example, picking up the victim's books and handing them to him or her;

- privately support those being hurt with words of kindness;

- express disapproval of bullying behavior by not joining in the laughter, teasing, or spreading of rumors or gossip.

Strategies for Parents

- Be careful not to convey to a child who is being victimized that something is wrong with him/her or that he/she deserves such treatment. All children are entitled to courteous and respectful treatment. Convince your child that he or she is not at fault and that the bully's behavior is the source of the problem.

- It is appropriate to call the school if your child is involved in a conflict as either a victim or a bully. Work collaboratively with the school personnel to address the problem. Keep records of incidents so that you can be specific in your discussions with school personnel about your child's experiences at school.

- You may wish to arrange a conference with a teacher, principal, or counselor. School personnel may be able to offer some practical advice to help you and your child.

- Offer support to your child but do not encourage dependence on you. Rescuing your child from challenges by assuming responsibility yourself when things are not going well does not teach your child independence. The more choices a child has to make, the more he or she develops independence, and independence can contribute to self-confidence.

- Do not encourage your child to be aggressive or to strike back. Rather, teach your child to be assertive. A bully often is looking for an indication that his/her threats and intimidation are working. Tears or passive acceptance only reinforces the bully's behavior. A child who does not respond, as the bully desires, is not likely to be chosen as a victim.

- If the problem persists or escalates, you may need to seek an attorney's help or contact local law enforcement officials. Violence or acts of bullying should not be tolerated in the school or in the community. Students should not have to tolerate bullying or violence at school any more than adults would tolerate such situations at work.

What Can Administrators Do to Prevent School Violence?

A school administrator can have a powerful effect on preventing school violence by focusing a laser-like light on the following items and demonstrating that he/she:

Creating a Situational Awareness

- is aware of informal groups and relationships among students in the school;
- is conscious of issues in the school that have not surfaced but could create violence;
- has the ability to predict what could go wrong from day-to-day;
- is sensitive to gang presence and/or drug use on or near the school site.

Intellectual Stimulation

- keeps well informed about current research and theory regarding all forms of school violence;
- continually exposes staff to cutting-edge ideas about how to effectively deal with bullying, fighting, drugs, alcohol, gangs;
- systematically engages staff in discussions about current research and theory;
- invites into the school/district experts on possible causes of and things schools can do to deal with the variety of school violence issues;
- continuously involves the staff in reading books and articles about effective practices;
- consciously challenges faculty, parents, and staff regarding the status quo;
- is comfortable with leading change initiatives with uncertain outcomes;
- systematically considers new and better ways of doing things.

Input

- provides opportunity for input on all-important decisions from all stakeholders;

- provides opportunities for staff to be involved in developing school policies (e.g., school safety plans);

- develops and uses a leadership team in decision-making.

Culture

- promotes cooperation among staff;

- promotes a sense of wellbeing;

- promotes cohesion among all students, staff, parents, and guests;

- insures that a positive school culture exists that supports school achievement.

(Adapted from *District Practices and Student Achievement: Lessons from Alberta.* Society for the Advancement of Excellence. Alberta, Canada: Patrick McGuire.)

Identifying Risk Factors for Students to Cause School Violence

Imagine if schools had some way of identifying potential students who might cause school violence. The Baton Rouge, Louisiana Partnership has identified seventeen risk factors. While this identification in no way predicts who might cause school violence, it can be used as a template.

Violence has reached epidemic proportions in Baton Rouge, with residents experiencing 11.96 violent crimes per 1,000 residents compared to an average of 6.88 violent crimes for the rest of the state. An even greater difference is evident if the figure from Baton Rouge is compared with the nationwide figure of 4.5 violent crimes per 1,000 people. The Baton Rouge Partnership for the Prevention of Juvenile Gun Violence targets the most chronic violent youths up to age 21 from two high-crime Zip code areas. This concept has helped enormously to mobilize the community to contribute in myriad ways to the program in order to help students overcome their problems. Nearly 300 community agencies and citizens are involved in some way. The Baton Rouge Partnership for the Prevention of Juvenile Gun Violence (a part of the Office of Juvenile Justice) has identified the risk factors for students ages 13–21 to cause school violence.

Risk Factors

Individual

- few social ties (involved in social activities, popularity)
- general delinquency involvement
- high alcohol/drug use
- illegal gun ownership/carrying
- physical violence/aggression
- violent victimization.

Family

- child maltreatment (abuse or neglect)
- delinquent/gang-involved siblings
- family history of problem behavior/criminal involvement
- family violence (child maltreatment, partner violence, conflict)
- poor parental supervision (control, monitoring, and child management).

School

- Frequent truancy/absences/suspensions; expelled from school; dropping out of school
- poor school attitude/performance; academic failure.

Community

- availability of firearms
- high-crime neighborhood.

Peer

- association with antisocial/aggressive/delinquent peers; high peer delinquency
- peer alcohol/drug use.

A comparison of recidivism rates between the identified group and a comparison group showed positive results. Forty-three percent of the treatment group was rearrested for a criminal offense during the monitoring period, compared with 72 percent of the comparison group. Sixteen percent of the treatment group was rearrested for a violent crime, compared with 41 percent of the comparison group. And 16 percent were rearrested for a gun-related crime, compared with 25 percent of the comparison group.

However, the evaluation of area-wide program effects was quite positive. An analysis of firearm offenses in Baton Rouge showed a decrease in firearm robberies in the target area during the three years following the start of the program. The average number dropped from 110 to ninety-two—a 16 percent decrease—while in the surrounding areas there was only a 6 percent decrease, from 105 to ninety-nine. This is a significant difference.

(Source: Department of Juvenile Services, East Baton Rouge Parish)

Identifying School Shooters

As a result of the shootings at Columbine High School in Colorado, the FBI and the United States Secret Service both investigated and issued two similar reports. The FBI's School Shooter Report and the Secret Service's National Threat Assessment Report (both issued in 2002) concluded that there isn't a profile to identify potential school shooters.

The researchers found that killers do not "snap." "They plan. They acquire weapons. These children take a long, considered, public path toward violence." Princeton's Katherine Newman has found that, far from being "loners," the perpetrators are "joiners" whose attempts at social integration fail, and that they let their thinking and even their plans be known, sometimes frequently over long periods of time. Many of the shooters told Secret Service investigators that alienation or persecution drove them to violence.

According to the United States Secret Service, instead of looking for traits, adults should ask about behavior:

- What has this child said?
- Do they have grievances?
- What do their friends know?
- Do they have access to weapons?
- Are they depressed or despondent?
- Have they been using antidepressant drugs that have a documented history of producing violence and aggression as a side effect?

Making an Emergency Preparedness Plan

Students, staff, and parents want a safe, stable environment in which to teach and learn. Therefore, school officials, in conjunction with a number of different stakeholders need to prepare an integrated, system-wide, closed-loop emergency preparedness plan.

Schools can be disrupted for a number of reasons and educators need to be prepared with a plan to address all possible disruptions or crises including crime, natural disasters, violence, terrorism, infrastructure failure (pipes busting, roof leaking), etc. These plans should be tailored to the school's size, grade levels, and geographic location. The risks can be divided into four categories:

- highly damaging and likely to happen (tornadoes in Oklahoma, earthquakes in California, hurricanes in Florida)
- minimally damaging, but likely to happen (monsoon winds in New Mexico and Arizona, flooding in Louisiana)
- highly damaging, but unlikely to happen (school shootings)
- minimally damaging and unlikely to happen.

Once categories are divided, the staff's roles and responsibilities need to be assessed. School administrators will want to delegate responsibilities in response in the following manner:

- **WHO:** is responsible for activating the emergency?
  Who contacts the media, parents, law enforcement, deals with rumors?

- **WHERE:** are students to be sent in the event of an emergency?

- **HOW:** are people to be notified? Phone systems (telephone tree)? Internet? Social media? School website? Text messaging? Fax?

- **WHEN:** is an emergency to be declared? Is a lockdown to be put in place? In middle and high schools, when is the bell system to be shut down so that students will remain in their classrooms and not wander the halls?

At a school with hundreds of students and almost a hundred staff, frequently in multiple buildings, an emergency preparedness plan will shorten the time to reach everyone with vital emergency information. The faculty needs to be made aware of what they are expected to do. Once staff are made aware of their individual responsibilities, this will reduce the natural panic when faced with an actual situation. Of course, this means that the plan needs to be deployed by testing it through holding a series of drills. Once tested, a group needs to study the results, adjust the plan to improve it, and remove shortcomings.

Two words of warning:

1 In the event of an actual emergency, school counselors need to be made available to students and staff to deal with stress and possible grief counseling.

2 Media and law enforcement officials should be given "code words" or phrases so that malicious individuals speaking in the name of the school do not give out false or spiteful information.

What Can Schools Do to Prevent Gang Involvement?

Young people of every socioeconomic and ethnic background participate in gangs. Although the majority of gang members are male, female gang involvement is growing. Gangs used to predominantly exist in the inner cities, but recently have expanded to suburbs and rural areas.

Why Do Young People Join Gangs?

Schools need to identify the causes of why children join gangs in order to prevent the formation of gang presence in schools.

- to have protection in and out of school
- to earn money
- because they seek excitement
- to obtain drugs and/or alcohol
- because gangs give "love" which is frequently missing from homes and parents
- gangs provide an identity
- peer pressure
- lack of school achievement
- to have a sense of belonging
- one of the strongest predictors of gang affiliation is a high level of interaction with antisocial peers.

Reasons Why Girls Join Gangs

While some of the reasons are similar, there are other reasons for joining gangs that are specific to girls:

- high rates of physical and sexual abuse
- self affirmation
- sense of power
- have family members, friends, or boyfriends that are involved with the gang
- protection
- aggressive nature and prone to fighting
- chronic delinquent and criminal experiences or records
- sense of belonging
- money and respect

- have needs that have been neglected or unmet: many girls use the gang as a replacement family and often find love and support within the gang
- desire for a family-structure environment
- forced by local gang members to join.

(Source: OJJDP's Girls Study Group)

Note: Not everyone with these characteristics belongs to a gang. Data is contradictory. Gang youth has been found in intact two-parent, single-parent, and recombined families. Gang members are not limited to homes in which parents have low educational achievement or low income.

What Schools Can Do

Anyone seeking to leave a gang must sincerely want to leave—no one can force them to quit. Anyone leaving, and those who support them, needs to understand that former enemies will still be enemies and he/she will no longer have the protection of the gang.

- Involve participation of all stakeholders working in collaboration to address the gang's challenges. Include law enforcement, school resource officers (SROs), teachers, administrators, parents, and students. School prevention and intervention programs cannot work outside the community, family, and law enforcement efforts. There needs to be a coordination of these efforts.
- Educate students about the dangers of joining gangs, as well as how to identify them. (Gang members wear particular items of clothing, such as bandanas or baseball caps of a specific color, or display gang-related tattoos or symbols. Gangs often use special hand signs or handshakes to tell others which gang they belong to.)
- Offer students an alternative to joining a gang. Such things as encouraging them to join a sports team or after-school club have been found to work as have after-school programs.
- Educate parents on the dangers of gang membership and provide parents with tips and tools on how to identify if their child is a gang member. Arrange presentations during PTA meetings or a special safety

event. Invite speakers with an expertise on gang violence like local law enforcement personnel.

- Train teachers and faculty about indicators of gang involvement and how to recognize and respond to it.

- Insure that the school's safety plan includes information about a comprehensive crime prevention strategy. Include such things as school patrols, closed-circuit television monitors in less visible areas of the school like the cafeteria, bus area. Establish anonymous crime reporting through the use of a "Suggestion Box."

- Reduce the visibility of gang membership in the school by implementing and enforcing a strict dress code and prohibit any clothing or symbols that suggest gang membership.

- Provide IDs to staff as well as students in order to identify intruders in the building.

- With law enforcement people, establish a drug-free, gun-free safe zone which allows students and parents to feel that they are protected.

- Create a staff position to serve as a "third ear." The function of this position is to provide a value-free listener to hear students' concerns about all forms of potential school violence. This adult needs to be someone whom the students trust and respect.

- Establish some form of a "hotline" to notify staff of potential school violence. Use a code word, established in advance, so that staff can know when potential violence or gangs are present.

- Have a single school spokesperson to present to the media and/or parents to prevent the spread of rumors regarding real or imagined school violence. In several of the schools in which I served, the "third ear" served as that person.

- Request gang identification training for all school personnel, including secretaries, security officers, and bus drivers, from local gang officers on an annual basis. The trainings should include visuals of local gang tattoos, clothing, and other identifiers.

- Rival gang members may encounter one another inside school property or in parking lots, so both areas require attention and security.

- In the event of a serious gang incident in the community, schools may wish to develop escalated security protocols that include locking down the building and classrooms.

How Parents Can Identify if Their Children Are Involved with Gangs

Parents play a pivotal role in keeping their children out of gangs. Parents can protect their children from gang activity by taking positive action such as monitoring their children's activities and fostering close relationships with them. However, parents often lack factual information about gangs. This section is designed to provide parents with information in order to recognize and prevent gang involvement. Young people who become involved in a gang may exhibit the following negative behaviors:

- withdrawing from family
- declining school attendance, performance, or behavior
- staying out late without reason
- unusual desire for secrecy
- confrontational behavior, such as talking back, verbal abuse, name calling, and disrespect for parental authority
- sudden negative opinions about law enforcement or adults in positions of authority (school officials or teachers)
- change in attitude about school, church, or other normal activities, or change in behavior at these activities
- unusual interest in one or two particular colors of clothing or a particular logo
- interest in gang-influenced music, videos, and movies
- use and practice of hand signals to communicate with friends
- particular drawings or gang symbols on schoolbooks, clothing, notebooks, or even walls
- drastic changes in hair or dress style and/or having a group of friends who have the same hair or dress style
- withdrawal from longtime friends and forming bonds with an entirely new group of friends
- suspected drug use, such as alcohol, inhalants, or narcotics
- the presence of firearms, ammunition, or other weapons on their person or in the home

- non-accidental physical injuries, such as being beaten, or injuries to hands and knuckles from fighting

- unexplained cash or goods, such as clothing or jewelry.

> (Source: *Parents' Guide to Gangs,* published by the Office of Juvenile Justice and Dropout Prevention)

Parental Involvement in School Safety

What Every Parent Should Know; What Every Parent Should Say

Since the horrific incident at Columbine High School and Sandy Hook Elementary School, parents have increasingly been encouraged to get involved in the school safety efforts being put forth by their children's schools. In working with many parents over the past two years, the Center for the Prevention of School Violence, a division of North Carolina's Department of Juvenile Justice and Delinquency Prevention, has learned that parents often do not know how to begin their involvement and often say they do not have the time to get involved. What the Center suggests is that the simplest and maybe the best form of involvement that parents can pursue is gaining knowledge about what their children's schools are doing in the arena of school safety and talking with their children about school safety.

Knowledge parents should gain about their children's school includes:

- **Knowing their children's school.** This means being informed about what the school is doing to establish and maintain a safe learning environment. This knowledge is important so parents can answer their children's questions and concerns with facts rather than myth.

- **Knowing their children.** This means that they should know what their children's typical behavior patterns are so that they will recognize when behaviors change. This allows for identification of warning signs.

- **Knowing warning signs.** These are the signals of potential problems.

- **Knowing how to intervene when warning signs present themselves.** Parents should have an understanding of how schools and community resources can be accessed should problems arise.

- **Knowing how to connect with their children.** Every parent–child relationship is unique. Parents must take the lead in developing a relationship that works for both and allows each to gain understanding and insight. With specific reference to the safe schools issue, parents need to understand how each of their children is thinking about the issue and address each with appropriate levels of concern and understanding. Especially on this issue, children will take cues from their parents. Parents need to remember this and act accordingly. Five points parents should say to their children about school safety include:

  - Explaining to their children what the facts are about school safety. Explaining to their children the steps their schools are taking to promote safety is important if their children ask questions.

  - Explaining the odds. The chances of being killed in schools are less than one in a million according to the US Department of Education. It is important to explain to children that schools are typically safe environments.

  - Explaining that everyone has a responsibility for making schools safe—even children. Everyone should take responsibility. If a child sees inappropriate behavior or hears about the possibility that such behavior might happen (e.g., hears that someone is going to bring a gun to school), the child has a responsibility to tell an adult at school or the parent him/herself.

  - Explaining that violence is not an acceptable solution to problems the children may be experiencing. Parents need to explicitly address this because of the many messages that children are exposed to from various components of society which communicate that violence may be an appropriate response. It is important that parents articulate that violence is wrong.

  - Explaining that they are ready to listen. Parents should ask questions about how their children are feeling about the safety of their schools, and they should ask their children about more than feelings but also about behaviors (e.g., are there places at school they avoid because they don't feel safe?). When asking the questions, it is then important that parents actively listen to the answers. If concerns are raised, parents need to follow up with the schools about them and keep their children informed about what is being done.

The Center for the Prevention of School Violence states that a measured approach that communicates appropriate levels of concern with knowledge is important. Parents need to communicate concerns without unduly raising levels of fear. A parent's desire to discuss this issue may not be mirrored by the child; parents therefore need to proceed cautiously with these conversations. They need to be informed and ready to discuss the issue but not so eager as to raise fears.

Preparing Children to Deal with National Crisis

Today children and schools need to be prepared to deal with a variety of disasters including floods, tornadoes, huricanes, and even acts of terrorism. The Guilford County Schools of Greensboro, North Carolina, has developed the handout shown in Box 6.1.

Box 6.1 *Preparing Children to Deal with National Crisis*

Emotional Responses

- Emotional responses vary in nature and severity from child to child. Nonetheless, there are some common ways in how children (and adults) feel when their lives are impacted by acts of terrorism.

- Fear: Fear may be the main reaction—fear for the safety of you and your family as well as those involved. A child's picture of terrorism may include a bomb dropped on their home. Their worries may seem unreasonable, but to them, they are quite possible. Children will hear rumors at school and may let their imaginations run wild. They may think the worst, however unrealistic it may be. The threat of further terrorism or war may also add to their fear. Other fears may be experienced as a result of media coverage (radio, television, newspapers). Fears or concerns may be about friends or relatives in the immediate vicinity of the terrorism.

- Loss of control: Terrorist actions are something over which children—and most adults—have no control. Lack of control can be overwhelming and confusing. Children may grasp at any control which they can have.

- Anger: Anger is not an unusual reaction. Unfortunately, anger is often expressed to those with whom children are most secure. Children may be angry at people in other countries for their acts of terrorism. Children should be allowed to express their feelings during this time.

- Loss of stability: Terrorism interrupts the natural order of things. It is very unsettling. Stability is gone, and this is very threatening. It can destroy trust and upset balance and a sense of security.

- Uncertainty: Children who have relatives or friends living in New York or Washington will be concerned that they do not know if their loved ones are safe. The lack of information over the next several days will only increase the uncertainty. If a child has suffered other losses or traumatic events, memories of those events may surface.

What Can I Do as a Parent?

- Acknowledge your children's feelings.

- Knowing what to say is often difficult. When no other words come to mind, a hug and saying, "This is really hard for you/us" may help.

- Try to recognize the feelings underlying your children's actions and put them into words. Say something like, "I can see you are feeling really scared about this."

- Recognize that your child may be fearful for his/her immediate safety. Reassure your child that the government, the military, and other adults are taking actions to ensure our safety.

- Sometimes children may have an overwhelming fear that they are unable to put into words that you may need to voice for them. For instance, if a parent is away, children may wonder what will become of them if the parent does not return. Try saying, "You never have to worry because we/you will be well taken care of. You won't be alone. Let me tell you our plan . . ."

- At times when your children are most upset, don't deny the seriousness of the situation. Saying to children, "Don't cry, everything will be okay," does not reflect how the child feels and does not make them feel better. Nevertheless, don't forget to express hope and faith that things will be alright.

- Older children in particular may need help identifying what they individually believe about war and terrorism. Questions such as "How could anyone do something like this?" may need discussion.

Help Your Children Put Their Fears in Perspective

- Help children to feel personally safe.

- Discuss what is realistic modern technology versus science fiction.

- Help children understand that precautions are being taken to prevent terrorism (e.g., bomb sniffing dogs, passport checks, heightened airport security) that might actually make them safer now than they usually are.

- Try to maintain normal routines to provide a sense of stability and security.

- Help children to feel a sense of control by taking some action.

- Send letters, cookies or magazines through relief agencies to those who have been impacted.

- If a family member gets called away, make plans for some special activities.

- Gathering with other families who are also missing a loved one helps provide support for you as well as for your children.

- Special parent and child time can provide an extra sense of security that might be badly needed. Let your child know that you will set aside a particular half-hour each day to play. Make the time as pleasant and child-centered as possible. Return phone calls later and make your child the real focus of that special time.

- Involve children in planning how to cope. Control and ownership are fostered when children help to plan strategies for dealing with a situation.

- Prepare for difficulties with children at night.

- Maintain regular bedtime routines such as storytime to provide a sense of security. Special stuffed animals or blankets may be especially important right now.

- Sit near your child until he/she falls asleep for a few nights. Gradually withdraw this support by checking back in two minutes and continuing to lengthen this time until your child feels secure again.

- A light may be needed in or near your child's room.

- Siblings may want to sleep in the same room until they feel more secure again.

- Don't let your children focus too much of their time and energy on news coverage of the terrorist attacks. If children are choosing to watch CNN News for hours each evening, find other activities for them. You may also need to watch the news less intensely and spend more time in alternative family activities.

- Use outside support services if your child has a severe reaction. Your school counselor, school social worker, or school psychologist can assist or provide names of other professionals trained to deal with children. Religious and community organizations and mental health providers are possible resources.

- Take time for yourself and try to deal with your own reactions to the situation as fully as possible. This, too, will help your children.

- Always be honest with your child and do not be afraid to talk to others about your fears and concerns.

(Source: Prepared by Guilford County Schools, Greensboro, North Carolina, adapted from "Children and War—Responding to Operation Desert Storm" by Debby Waddell and Alex Thomas, in *Helping Children Grow Up in the 90's: A Resource Book for Parents and Teachers* by the National Association of School Psychologists (NASP))

7 Sexual Activity

There are few areas more controversial in our society and culture than teen pregnancy. The debate is raging about whether educators should address the issue and whether the conversation should center on abstinence, contraceptive education, or a combination of both (comprehensive sex education). The sides in this debate have been drawn along political and religious lines, and emotions run high on both sides. In addition, some educators feel uncomfortable discussing such things as condoms, sexually transmitted diseases, and pregnancy, feeling it is a parental responsibility.

I recently read that a 9-year-old girl gave birth in Mexico. She was impregnated at age 8 by a 14-year-old boy. Scientists are unsure what is causing children at increasingly younger ages to become fertile, grow breasts, and pubic hair. What is less surprising is that children are becoming progressively sexually active at younger and younger ages. What used to be of concern to high school educators is now becoming a concern to middle and elementary school educators. We now have children who are having and raising children, raising themselves, and raising their parents.

The United States has the highest rate of teen pregnancy in the fully industrialized world. The teen pregnancy in the US rate is ten times that of Japan, four times those of France and Germany, and nearly twice that of the UK. Although teen births continue to fall in the United States, they remain much higher than in most of the rest of the developed world. What is more discouraging is the fact that sexually transmitted infections (STIs) are seen in more than half of all Americans aged 15–24. About

9.5 million adolescents and young adults (ages 15–24) are diagnosed with sexually transmitted diseases (STDs) each year. An estimated four in ten sexually active adolescent females between the ages of 14 and 19 have an STD–www.hhs.gov/ash/oah/resources-and-publications/info/parents/just-facts/stds.html-_ftn2. In 2008, males accounted for an estimated 71 percent of all HIV diagnoses among adolescents aged 13–19.

(Source: US Department of Human Health and Services,
Office of Adolescent Services, www.hhs.gov/ash/oah/
resources-and-publications/info/parents/just-facts/stds.html)

As teens and pre-teens begin dating early, there has been a dramatic growth in dating violence as well as date rape. Adolescent dating violence is one of the strongest predictors of intimate partner violence, may lead to violence in adults, and is associated with injuries and health-compromising behaviors, such as unsafe sex, substance use, and suicide attempts. For adolescents, physical dating violence can be defined as acts ranging from threats of harm to punching or hitting with an object, and often emerges during stressful transition periods that involve new pressures and responsibilities for handling conflict and emotions in unfamiliar contexts. Nationally representative studies of physical dating violence victimization since the mid-1990s indicate that approximately one in ten to one in five high-school-aged teens are hit, slapped, or beaten by a dating partner each year (Centers for Disease Control and Prevention, *2011 Youth Risk Behavior Survey*, www.cdc.gov/violenceprevention/intimatepartnerviolence/teen_dating_violence.html). Anyone—regardless of gender, ethnicity, upbringing, or socioeconomic background—can be a victim of abuse in dating relationships.

Schools are impacted because of these behaviors. There are a variety of physical as well as emotional injuries, including unsafe sex, substance abuse, and suicide attempts, that are seen in schools. Chlamydia is the most commonly reported infectious disease in the United States. Gonorrhea is the second most commonly reported infectious disease in the country.

Schools need to determine what their role is in addressing teen pregnancy, date rape, and sexually transmitted diseases. Educators have the power to shift the focus from prevailing societal attitudes about these issues by providing access to education for their young, vulnerable charges.

Background

According to RAINN (Rape, Abuse & Incest National Network, www.rainn. org/) 207,754 Americans (ages 12 and older) are victims of sexual violence each year. And according to the Centers for Disease Control and Prevention (CDC):

- 60.4 percent of female and 69.2 percent of male victims were first raped before age 18.

- 25.5 percent of females were first raped before age 12, and 34.9 percent were first raped between the ages of 12 and 17.

- Among high school students surveyed nationwide, about 8 percent reported having been forced to have sex. The percentage of those having been forced to ever have sex was higher among female (11 percent) than male (5 percent) students.

- A 2005 survey of high school students found that 10.8 percent of girls and 4.2 percent of boys from grades 9–12 were forced to have sexual intercourse at some time in their lives.

- In the first rape experiences of female victims, perpetrators were reported to be intimate partners (30.4 percent), family members (23.7 percent), and acquaintances (20 percent).

- In the first rape experiences of male victims, perpetrators were reported to be acquaintances (32.3 percent), family members (17.7 percent), friends (17.6 percent), and intimate partners (15.9 percent).

- Young women between the ages of 14 and 17 represent 38 percent of those victimized by date rape.

- Rapes by acquaintances account for 60 percent of all rapes reported to rape crisis centers.

- Meanwhile, the average age at which teens begin having sex—16—hasn't changed in twenty years.

- HIV rates are also skyrocketing among specific populations, such as gay black youth. Nearly 6 percent of gay black men under 30 are newly infected with the AIDS virus each year. According to a study one in four black gay men are infected by age 25.

- Research now strongly links HIV infection in the US with poverty and social issues such as homelessness, incarceration, lack of education, racial discrimination, and homophobia.

- One in ten young women have sex before the age of 15.

- About half of all teens report they are sexually active. Only 60 percent of those having sex use condoms. Sixty-six percent of females and 71 percent of males use condoms at first intercourse. Because of the faulty and sporadic use of contraception, a significant number of those having intercourse become pregnant.

- Thirty-four percent of teenage girls in the US are becoming pregnant at least once before the age of 20.

- Almost half (48 percent) of all non-marital first births are to teen parents (source: National Campaign to Prevent Teen Pregnancy, "Why it Matters: Teen Pregnancy, Out-of-Wedlock Births, Healthy Relationships and Marriage," 2006, www.thenationalcampaign.org/why-it-matters/pdf/marriage.pdf).

> (Source: "Sexual Violence: Facts at a Glance," 2008, www.
> cdc.gov/ViolencePrevention/pdf/sv-datasheet-a.pdf, and
> "Understanding Sexual Violence: Fact Sheet," 2012, www.
> cdc.gov/violenceprevention/pdf/SV_factsheet-a.pdf)

The 2002 National Survey of Family Growth (NSFG, www.cdc.gov/nchs/nsfg.htm), conducted by the CDC, provided relevant national statistics on other sexual activities:

- At ages 15–19 more teens reported having had oral sex than sexual intercourse.

- Teens who have sex at an early age are less likely than older teens to use contraception the first time they have sex.

- Approximately one-third of all teen pregnancies end in an induced abortion.

What Schools Can Do to Prevent Student Pregnancy

Many children, even teens, have incorrect information about sex and pregnancy. Some believe that the first time they have sex they cannot become pregnant. Others believe that if they have sex while they have their period, they will not become pregnant. Many believe that "being in love" means "making love." Since sexual activity precedes pregnancy, schools need to stress to students the importance of taking effective measures in reducing and preventing youth pregnancy.

There are a number of things that schools can do to give students the help to prevent student pregnancy:

- It is never too early to develop sex education curriculum. Age-appropriate sex education should start in the kindergarten and continue through 12th grade.

- Schools can do much more by, for example, facilitating access to childcare and transportation, flexible scheduling for pregnant students, individualized graduation plans, supportive mentors and counselors.

- Parents should be notified and informed of their options and be given choices for consent in having their children in classes where contraception is taught.

- Schools can provide comprehensive, medically accurate, and age-appropriate sex education and referrals to family-planning services.

- The curriculum should include topics such as abstinence, relationships, decision-making, pregnancy, and sexually transmitted diseases.

- Teaching self-esteem should be part of the curriculum.

- Schools should teach young males that they also have a responsibility for teen pregnancy.

- The curriculum should be taught by sensitive, respected, and honest teachers.

- The curriculum should be openly discussed with all staff prior to implementation.

What Counselors Should Know about Teen Sexuality and Pregnancy

The information below will serve as a refresher for some counselors. For some administrators, other support personnel, and teachers this information may be new.

Early childbearing compounds the poverty and low educational attainment that are the precursors of teen pregnancy. Compared to their peers who postpone childbearing, teenage mothers tend to have:

- more psychological problems
- lower graduation rates
- less stable employment
- greater reliance on social assistance and welfare
- higher poverty rates
- more marital instability
- more frequent health problems.

Research findings show that the babies of teen mothers also suffer:

- Children born to teen mothers receive less medical care, partly because many teen mothers have no health insurance.
- Children of teen mothers are 50 percent more likely to repeat a grade, under-perform in standardized tests, and less likely to complete a high school degree than children of older mothers.
- Reported incidents of abuse and neglect of children are twice as common in families headed by a teen mother than in families in which childbearing has been delayed until the mother is in her early twenties.
- Teens growing up in families disrupted by divorce and remarriage tend to have intercourse at an earlier age.
- Earlier onset of sexual activity correlates with low parental monitoring, as well as with permissive sexual attitudes and behavior in parents.
- Sexually active adolescents have been found to perform more poorly in school, start dating earlier than their peers, and have more friends encouraging sexual experimentation.
- Early sexual activity has been linked to a greater number of sexual partners over time and an increased risk of teen pregnancy and sexually transmitted infections.
- The younger a girl is when she becomes sexually active, the more likely she will end up pregnant as a teenager.
- Sexual activity during adolescence has been associated with a host of risk-taking activities, including substance use and delinquency.

Scenarios to Prevent Dating Violence

Adolescent dating violence is one of the strongest predictors of adult partner relationship abuse (*Teen Dating Violence: A Literature Review and Annotated Bibliography,* www.ncjrs.gov/pdffiles1/nij/grants/235368. pdf) and is associated with injuries and health-compromising behaviors such as unsafe sex, substance abuse, and suicide attempts. Schools may wish to assist young people in dealing with these challenges by working with potential scenarios. A few examples are listed below. Pre-teens and teenagers are capable of making good decisions with the help of others. Counselors might want to have youngsters develop some scenarios of their own. These might deal with rape, sexually transmitted disease, pregnancy, or prostitution.

- A girl who has met an older boy online finally has a chance to see him, at his house, alone. What might happen if she does?
- A boy with a longtime girlfriend goes to a party out of town, where another girl flirts with him and invites him over. What might be the consequences?
- Your girlfriend threatens suicide if you leave her. What do you do?
- An older family friend makes some sexual overtures to you. What should you do?
- Your boyfriend wants you to send nude pictures of yourself over the Internet as proof that you love him. Should you do it?
- Your boyfriend hits you when he sees you talking with another boy. What do you do?

Fifteen Rape Myths

Many educators have heard stories from students about what they have heard from their friend about rape. Here are a few of the myths and the factual realities. It is important that teachers and counselors educate young people about the risks and precautions they can take to prevent rape. I suggest that the following be used as a quiz for students and parents.

The Rape Myth Quiz[1]

According to RAINN (Rape, Abuse and Incest National Network, www. rainn.org/) 207,754 Americans (ages 12 and older) are victims of sexual violence each year.

1 "She Gave Her Permission. It Wasn't Rape"

The age of consent varies by state. In most of the United States the age of consent is 16 to 18. Anything younger is statutory rape.

2 Rape Is Always about Sex

Rape is a life-threatening experience. One out of every eight adult women has been a victim of forcible rape (National Victim Center and Crime Victims Research and Treatment Center, 1992, www.ncdsv.org/images/national statisticssexassault—afreport8–24–05.pdf). Gratification comes from gaining power and control and discharging anger. Many rapists never achieve sexual gratification. For those who do, this gratification is only temporary, so the rapist seeks another victim. Rape is an act of violence, not passion. It is an attempt to hurt and humiliate, using sex as the weapon.

3 Women by Wearing Sexy, Suggestive Clothing Incite Men to Rape

Research has found that the vast majority of rapes are planned (University of Minnesota Duluth, www.d.umn.edu/cla/faculty/jhamlin/3925/myths.html).

---

1 Statistics were obtained from various sources including the study *Rape in America,* 1992; National Victim Center, RAINN (Rape, Abuse and Incest National Network), www.rainn. org/; the Federal Bureau of Investigation (FBI); the National Crime Survey; and the CDC; "List of Rape Myths" by John Hamlin (University of Minnesota Duluth, retrieved 6/21/2006, www.d.umn.edu/cla/faculty/jhamlin/3925/myths.html); www.HopeforHealing.org (retrieved 11/22/2013); the *VAASA Volunteer Manual, Second Edition* (2006); and the Project Horizon Website (retrieved 5/22/2006, http://organizations.rockbridege.net/projecthorizon/ sacommonmyths.htm).

Rape is the responsibility of the rapist alone. In fact, women and girls have been raped while wearing everything from pajamas to jeans to business clothing.

4 Most Rapes Occur in a Dark Alley by a Stranger

Most victims of rape know their attacker. Someone they know—boyfriends, family members, close neighbors, relatives, or dates–commit about 75 percent of rapes. There is no common profile of a rapist. People of all economic levels, all races, and all occupations commit rape. A rapist can be your doctor, your clergyman, a lawyer, or a police officer. Rape can and does occur anytime and anyplace. Many rapes occur during the day and in the victims' homes. Seventy-one percent of rapes are planned in advance. Sixty percent of convicted rapists were married or had regular sexual partners at the time of the assault. The majority of reported rapes occur either in the victim's home or the home of the attacker. In many cases, the victim met the offender in a public place and then was coerced into accompanying the rapist to the place of the assault.

5 Myth: There Is a "Right Way" to Respond to a Rape Situation

Since rape is life-threatening and each rapist has his own pattern, the best thing a victim can do is follow her instincts and observe any cues from the rapist. If the victim escapes alive she has done the right thing. Many rapists carry a weapon and threaten the victim with violence or death.

6 Myth: A Victim Should Be Discouraged from Dwelling on the Rape. She/He Should "Forget It"

All victims should be offered the opportunity to talk about the assault with those personally close to them and knowledgeable professionals. Victims who are not allowed to talk about the rape have a much more difficult time recovering from it.

7 Myth: Rapists Are Non-White. Rapists Are Lower Class. Rapists Are "Criminal Types"

Rapists are not physically identifiable. They may appear friendly, normal, and non-threatening. Many are young, married, and have children. A rapist can be anyone: doctor, policeman, clergyman, social worker, or corporate president.

8 Myth: Men Can't Be Raped

There were approximately 20,000 sexual assaults of males ages 12 and over in the United States in 1991 (Bureau of Justice statistics, 1992).

9 Myth: Incest Is Rare

Incest is common and happens in every community. An estimated 77 percent of reported sexual abusers are parents (57 percent of the total being natural parents), 16 percent are other relatives, and 6 percent are non-related (Thoringer et al., 1988, "Prevention of Child Sexual Abuse," *School Psychology Review* 17(4): 614–636).

10 Myth: Sexual Assaults Affect Few People. After All, No One I Know Has Been Raped

Sexual assaults are very common. Most victims are reluctant to discuss their assaults and many succeed in totally blocking the assault from conscious memory. An estimated 155,000 women were raped each year between 1973 and 1987 (US Department of Justice, 1991).

11 Myth: Women Often Make False Reports of Rape

Fact: Rape can and does strike anyone at anytime. Age, social class, and/ or ethnic group has no bearing on the person a rapist chooses to attack. Research data clearly proves that the way a woman dresses and/or acts does not influence the rapist's choice of victims. His decision to rape is based on how easily he perceives his target can be intimidated. Rapists are looking for available and vulnerable targets.

The FBI reports that only 2 percent of rape reports are given falsely. This is the same report rate as for other felonies.

12 Myth: If the Assailant, Victim, or Both Are Drunk and Use Drugs, the Assailant Cannot Be Charged with Rape

Forcing sex on someone who is too drunk to give consent is second-degree rape in North Carolina. (It carries a prison sentence of up to seventeen years.) People who commit crimes while under the influence of alcohol or drugs are not considered free from guilt. The fact that a woman has been drinking does not imply consent. Alcohol and drugs can render a woman incapable of consent.

13 Myth: Gang Rape Is Rare

In 43 percent of all reported cases, more than one assailant was involved.

14 Myth: Rape Does Not Have Any Lasting Effect on the Victim

After being raped: 42 percent of women reported feeling afraid of men; 28 percent said it affected their sex lives; 27 percent felt less independent or more afraid of being on their own; 28 percent said it damaged their trust in male–female relationships; 18 percent felt worthless or lost self-respect; 17 percent felt hostile toward men; 10 percent sustained physical injuries; 7 percent reported suicidal impulses; 5 percent suffered nightmares.

15 Myth: If a Woman Agrees to Some Degree of Sexual Intimacy, She Wants to Have Sexual Intercourse

Fact: Any person has the right to agree to any degree of sexual intimacy they feel comfortable with at that moment, and to not go any further if they do not wish to. A person may feel comfortable with one kind of sexual activity but not wish another—or s/he may decide s/he's not really ready for further intimacy.

Helping Victims of Rape

There are many ways that you can help a friend or family member who has been a victim of rape or sexual violence:

- Listen. Be there. Don't be judgmental.
- Be patient. Remember, it will take your loved one some time to deal with the crime.
- Help to empower your loved one. Rape and sexual violence are crimes that take away an individual's power; it is important not to compound this experience by putting pressure on your loved one to do things that he or she is not ready to do yet.
- If you are dealing with an issue involving your child, create a safe place by talking directly to them.
- If you are the non-abusing parent in a case of incest, it is important to support your child and help them through this situation without blaming them. This is also true if you are not a parent but still an observer of incest.
- If your loved one is considering suicide, check up with them on a regular basis.
- Encourage your loved one to report the rape or sexual violence to law enforcement (call 911 in most areas). If your loved one has questions about the criminal justice process, talking with someone on the National Sexual Assault Hotline, 1.800.656.HOPE can help.
- Let your loved one know that professional help is available through the National Sexual Assault Hotline, 1.800.656.HOPE, and the National Sexual Assault Online Hotline.
- If your loved one is willing to seek medical attention or report the assault, offer to accompany him or her wherever s/he needs to go (hospital, police station, campus security, etc.).
- Encourage him or her to contact one of the hotlines, but realize that only your loved one can make the decision to get help.

(Source: RAINN)

8 | Suicide

Suicide is the third leading cause of death for 15- to 24-year-olds, according to the Centers for Disease Control and Prevention (CDC), after accidents and homicide. Almost as many teens die from suicide as the fourth through the tenth leading causes of death combined. It's also thought that at least twenty-five attempts are made for every completed teen suicide. Students who are bullied frequently feel that suicide is the only way to escape the taunting. Students who are gay or made to feel different because they are short, or too fat, or too skinny, or whatever resort to suicide.

If you've ever been in a school where a student has attempted or been successful in committing suicide, you know how devastating are the effects it has on other students, parents, friends of the victim, and staff. Schools report that there are frequently "copy cat" attempts after a reported successful attempt.

Suicide among young people is preventable—it just requires recognition and resources. Most schools have a written protocol for dealing with students who show signs of suicidal behavior. Unfortunately, many educators do not know the signs that indicate a potential suicide nor have they been trained in how to address the problem. Like many of the other social ills that schools are forced to deal with, suicide is something that schools must be proactive about.

Background

Did You Know?

- In the next 24 hours 1,439 teens will attempt suicide. As many as 250,000 adolescents made a serious unsuccessful effort to kill themselves last year.

- The fastest-growing group completing suicide is children between the ages of 10 and 14. Between 1981 and 2006, suicide rates increased by over 50 percent.

- The suicide rate in the past twenty-five years has been decreasing, yet the rate for those between 15 and 24 has tripled. The adolescent suicide rate is nearly 33 percent higher than that of the overall population.

- The ratio of male to female suicides is four to one. However young women attempt suicide nine times more frequently. Guns are the most common means of suicide among males. Pills are the most commonly used method of suicide for females.

- White males have had the highest increase in suicide, which rose 50 percent between 1970 and 1978. The incidence for white females increased 12 percent. Suicide among young blacks has also dramatically increased.

- Half of all children who have made one suicide attempt will make another, sometimes as many as two a year until they succeed.

- According to a study published in *Pediatrics,* gay and bisexual teens are 20 percent more likely to attempt suicide in politically conservative areas than in "supportive" environments.

- The risk of suicide increases dramatically when kids and teens have access to firearms at home, and nearly 60 percent of all suicides in the United States are committed with a gun. That's why any gun in a home should be unloaded, locked, and kept out of the reach of children and teens.

- Overdose using over-the-counter, prescription, and non-prescription medicine is also a very common method for both attempting and completing suicide. It's important to monitor carefully all medications in your home. Also be aware that teens will "trade" different prescription medications at school and carry them (or store them) in their locker or backpack.

- Native American suicide rates for ages 15–24 are three times that of all Americans in that age group according to the New Mexico Department of Health Data (Albuquerque Journal, November 19, 2011, p. C1).

(Source: National Alliance on Mental Health, www.nami.org/ Content/ContentGroups/Helpline1/Teenage_Suicide.htm)

Recognizing Risk Factors for Teenage Suicide

There are five general risk factors to identify people who are at risk of attempting suicide.

1   **Physical signs:** fatigue, repeated health complaints, red and glazed eyes, and a lasting cough.

2   **Emotional signs:** personality change, sudden mood changes, irritability, irresponsible behavior, low self-esteem, poor judgment, depression, and a general lack of interest.

3   **Family-influenced signs:** starting arguments, breaking rules, or withdrawing from the family.

4   **School signs:** decreased interests, negative attitude, drop in grades, many absences, truancy, and discipline problems.

5   **Social problems:** new friends who are less interested in standard home and school activities, problems with the law, and changes to less conventional styles in dress and music.

People who are most at risk of attempting suicide are those who:

- have made previous attempts
- have a family history of suicide
- have had a recent stressful event or loss in their lives
- have easy access to lethal weapons, especially guns
- have suffered a divorce or separation in their family
- are part of the formation of a new family with step-parents and step-siblings
- have moved to a new community, which can be very unsettling and can intensify self-doubts
- are experiencing a change in eating and sleeping habits
- have a noticeable withdrawal from friends, family, and regular activities
- exhibit violent actions, rebellious behavior, or running away

- use drugs and alcohol
- show an unusual neglect of personal appearance
- demonstrate marked personality change
- reveal persistent boredom, difficulty concentrating, or a decline in the quality of schoolwork
- frequently complain about physical symptoms, often related to emotions, such as stomachaches, headaches, fatigue, etc.
- show a loss of interest in pleasurable activities
- are not able to tolerate praise or rewards
- complain of being a bad person or feeling rotten inside
- give verbal hints with statements such as: "I won't be a problem for you much longer, Nothing matters, It's no use, and I won't see you again"
- put their affairs in order, for example, give away favorite possessions, clean their room, throw away favorite belongings
- become suddenly cheerful after a period of depression
- have signs of psychosis (hallucinations or bizarre thoughts)
- show disruptive school behavior
- demonstrate extreme personality changes
- show loss of interest in activities that used to be enjoyable
- have significant loss or gain in appetite
- have difficulty falling asleep or want to sleep all day
- experience fatigue or loss of energy
- express feelings of worthlessness or guilt
- withdraw from family and friends
- neglect their personal appearance or hygiene
- show sadness, irritability, or indifference
- are having trouble concentrating
- show extreme anxiety or panic
- use or abuse drugs and/or alcohol
- show aggressive, destructive, or defiant behavior

- perform poorly in school

- experience hallucinations or have unusual beliefs

- have suffered a major disappointment, rejection, failure, or loss, such as breaking up with a girlfriend or boyfriend, failing a big exam, or witnessing family turmoil.

While these are warning signs, they are not all of the possible signs. Suffering from one of these symptoms certainly does not necessarily mean that a person is suicidal.

If a child or adolescent says, "I want to kill myself," or "I'm going to commit suicide," always take the statement seriously and immediately seek assistance from a qualified mental health professional. Make it clear that you care; stress your willingness to listen. An estimated 80 percent of all those who commit suicide give some warning of their intentions or mention their feelings to a friend or family member.

Not all suicide attempts lead to successful suicides.

(Source: National Youth Violence Prevention Resource Center and American Academy of Child and Adolescent Psychiatry, www.acap.org)

What Are the Causes of Youth Suicide?

- **Depression:** A teen that is feeling suicidal may see no other way out of their problems, no other escape from emotional pain or no one to whom they can communicate how they feel. Depression expresses itself in a variety of ways including: changes in appetite; changes in activity level; loss of sleep; lack of interest in activities that normally give pleasure; social withdrawal; and thoughts of death or punishment.

- **Substance abuse problems:** Alcohol and some drugs are depressants. Youths who are depressed may take these substances thinking that they will help ease the pain. In reality, they make the situation worse. They may limit their ability to assess risk, cloud their judgment, make good choices, and think of solutions to their problems.

- **Teenage stress:** There are many pressures on teenagers—ones that they have never experienced before. These include social, academic, personal, sexual, and relationship pressures. Some teens struggle with weight and eating problems, while others face learning difficulties in school. Getting in trouble in school or with the law and fighting with parents are risk factors for suicide. A traumatic event like a breakup, failing a test, an unintended pregnancy, or getting into an accident can bring on suicidal tendencies.

- **Violence:** There is more violence in the newspapers, on television, in electronic games, and in the movies. Many children live in increasingly violent neighborhoods. There is increased violence in homes including familial violence and sexual abuse. And it is easier to get the tools (guns and pills) of suicide. Young people are five times more likely to commit suicide if they live in a home in which there is a gun.

- **Lack of parental engagement:** Many children grow up in single-parent households. Others have two working parents. According to one study, 90 percent of suicidal teenagers believed their families did not understand them. Data show that families are spending less time together and more of our young people are spending more and more time in front of television and computer screens.

What Can Educators Do to Prevent Youth Suicide?

- While no one single symptom—or even a combination of factors—is a predictor of suicide, **if they suspect that a student is suicidal, teachers and students should tell a counselor or an administrator.**

- **Always take suicidal comments very seriously.** If a student says that he or she is thinking about suicide, you need to take him or her seriously. If you assume that the person is only seeking attention, you may be making a serious and potentially fatal decision.

- **Listen attentively to everything that a potential suicidal person has to say.** Encourage the person talk as much as he or she wants to. Listen closely so that you can be as supportive as possible, and learn as much as possible about what is the cause of the pain.

- **Comfort the person with words of encouragement.** There is no script to follow in these situations.

- **Don't lecture or point out all the reasons a person has to live.** Instead, **listen** and reassure the individual that depression and suicidal tendencies can be treated.

- **If you suspect that the individual is at high risk of suicide, do not leave the person alone.** If you are in doubt, call 911.

- **Know your limits.** Most of us have not been trained in how to handle situations like this. Be supportive; listen attentively; let the person know that you are deeply concerned.

- **There are a number of local suicides "hotlines."** Their numbers are listed in your local telephone directories. Check the numbers at the front of your telephone directory or call the emergency numbers. There is a national Suicide Helpline-1800-SUICIDE. These telephone lines are staffed 24 hours a day, seven days a week by trained professionals who can help without ever needing to know the name of the individual calling. All calls are confidential.

Helping Children Survive a Family Crisis

America's children are probably under greater stress today than any previous generation of children. They need to deal not only with the pressures listed below but also with the economic slowdown and its impact on the family: the problems of coming up with money to pay for college, etc.

Sometimes day-to-day hassles can pile up and cause a stress overload on children that they and their family do not recognize. At other times something unexpected can occur.

The following events can stress young people:

- someone dies

- their house burns down

- a family member loses a job

- a family member gets married

- a family member gets divorced

- puberty

- families merging
- parent(s) retiring
- a parent cheating on a partner
- feeling suicidal
- alcoholism in the family
- physical and/or sexual abuse
- drug use
- disagreement over parental attitudes towards use of television, cell phones, tattoos, body piercings, etc.
- perceived inflexibility of parents' attitude toward dating partner.

When a child is immobilized by stress this may manifest itself in the following ways:

- depression
- loss of appetite
- anxiety
- striking out
- hostility
- criticism of others
- weight loss
- weight gain
- tattooing
- body piercings
- shortness of temper
- misbehaving more than usual
- seeking attention
- having trouble sleeping
- crying
- feeling worried and concerned about family problems
- problems in school, such as fighting or not paying attention
- falling grades.

What Schools Can Do

- Schools can develop and supply a list of outside resources providing professional help that parents and students can access.

- Schools can develop a School–Family Support Team which can provide a strong, social, supportive network providing assistance to young people who seek help.

- Counselors, social workers, and other support personnel can recognize the warning signs in young people.

- Schools can provide a "third ear" to listen to youngsters.

- They can provide an environment that allows students to talk openly and honestly about their families and their lives without condemnation.

- They can encourage young people to be optimistic without denying the reality of the situation(s).

What Schools Can Do to Stop Bullying of Those Who Are Perceived to Be Different

There is a great deal of harassment of those who are perceived to be different. Those who are harassed may be small for their age, pretty, non-athletic, overweight or plump, or have physical or mental defects. No group has been more harassed than those who have a real or perceived non-heterosexual orientation. Lesbian, gay, bisexual, and transgender (LGBT) youth are subjected to slurs at school and sometimes assaulted. They are often told that they are sinners. Some are told to kill themselves for being gay and that being gay is a sin against God. They have been urinated upon, stabbed in the neck, pushed into school lockers and walls.

The evidence on LGBT suicides is mixed. The National Action Alliance for Suicide Prevention (http://actionallianceforsuicideprevention. org/) notes there are no national data (for the US) regarding suicidal ideation or suicide rates among LGBT youth. It is believed that the suicide rate is comparatively higher than that of the general population. However, there is no agreed percentage of the national population that is LGBT, or that identifies as LGBT, and death certificates do not include information about sexuality. The Suicide Prevention Resource Center (www.sprc. org/) estimates that between 30 and 40 percent of LGBT youth, depending on age and sex groups, have attempted suicide. A US government study, titled "Report of the Secretary's Task Force on Youth Suicide" (http://eric.ed.gov/?id=ED33450), published in 1989, found that LGBT youth are four times more likely to attempt suicide than other young people.

A 2009 survey by the CDC of more than 7,000 LGBT middle and high school students aged 13–21 years found that in the past year, because of their sexual orientation:

- eight out of ten students had been verbally harassed at school;
- six out of ten felt unsafe at school; and
- one in five had been the victim of a physical assault at school.

The following are recommended steps that schools can take:

- Identify outside agencies that may be able to help.
- Fully investigate reports of harassment and bullying.
- Provide support for those who are bullied and their parents.
- Notify law enforcement in case this is a violation of state or local laws.
- Take action to address hostile school climates that target LGBT students.
- Develop procedures for notifying parents while maintaining sensitivity to a student's right of privacy.
- Designate a staff member who will develop a harassment prevention program to eliminate and prevent future harassment.
- Designate a qualified mental health professional to be available during school hours for students in need.

9 Truancy and Suspension

Contrary to popular belief, truancy cuts across all student demographics. Truants live in rural and urban school districts and represent all races.

Students who do not come to school do not learn, miss critical instruction for understanding key concepts, and fall behind quickly in completing assignments. Good school attendance often correlates positively to good academic achievement. Students who are truant from school often drop out of school later. Dropping out limits students' future alternatives, both in getting a higher education and getting a job. Coming to school every day, being on time, and completing daily school assignments are all job-related skills. Students who attend school regularly and complete their schoolwork on time are more prepared to be regular in their work attendance and more able to complete their work duties as adults. Research indicates that the greatest predictor of school success is children's attendance in school.

What do students who are chronically truant do? What do these students do when they are not in school? A child who does not attend school has a capacity to be involved in other not necessarily positive behaviors like taking drugs, committing crimes, or becoming involved in sexual activities.

While high school juniors and seniors have the highest absentee rates, truancy begins in elementary school, and it becomes an established behavior by the end of 9th grade. The Boston Channel (www.wcvb.com/) reported that in Massachusetts 2,210 *pre-k–3rd grade students* (my emphasis) were suspended in the 2009–2010 school year. According to the *CT* (Connecticut) *Mirror* (www.ctmirror.org/story/2013/05/17/hundreds-kindergarten-students-suspended-school), there were 1,967 incidents of students *age 6 and under* (my emphasis) that were suspended last school year—almost all of them black or Hispanic. According to a report from the Connecticut Department of

Education, the number of students suspended is actually higher, but privacy issues restrict the state agency from releasing information that could identify unique student information. Early intervention is the key in order to prevent pupils from developing the habit. Nearly half of truant students surveyed said they were absent about once a week or more. Fifteen percent of all students— about seven million—miss a month or more of school each year.

How can students learn if they are not in school? In schools across the country, out-of-school suspensions have become the default punishment not only for drugs and fights but also for threats, displays of affection, dress code violations, truancy, tardiness, refusal to follow directions, even 4-year-olds' temper tantrums.

Are schools perpetuating underachievement by suspending students? Schools have to balance suspension against possible alternatives. They have to provide safe environments for all of the other students. Students should be suspended if they are harming themselves or stopping the learning of others. But who is being punished? How many are being punished and for what kinds of infractions? Schools may actually encourage truancy by a "one-size-fits-all punishment philosophy" called zero tolerance. Suspending students for minor offenses like having prescription drugs which parents send in to school with their child doesn't make sense.

Background

Truancy

- Chronic truancy and absence (which includes excused and unexcused absences) often start early. For instance, it is reported that 20 percent of elementary school students (90,000) in New York City schools missed at least a month of school during the 2007–2008 school year (K. Nauer, A. White, and R. Yerneni, 2008, *Strengthening Schools by Strengthening Families: Community Strategies to Reverse Chronic Absenteeism in the Early Grades and Improve Supports for Children and Families,* Center for New York City Affairs).

- Data from the Baltimore (MD) Education Research Project showed that more than one-third of the 1st-grade cohort was chronically absent (that is, missed one or more months of schooling in one year) during at least one of the first five years in school (Balfanz et al., 2008).

- The costs of truancy are high. Truancy has been clearly identified as one of the early warning signs that youths are potentially headed for delinquent activity, social isolation, or educational failure. As a risk factor for delinquent behavior in youth, truancy has been found to be related to substance abuse, gang activity, and involvement in criminal activities such as burglary, auto theft, and vandalism (M. L. Baker, J. N. Sigmon, and M. E. Nugent, 2001, "Truancy Reduction: Keeping Students in School," *Juvenile Justice Bulletin,* September, www.ncjrs. gov/pdffiles1/ojjdp/188947.pdf).

- Every year as many as seventy-five million students nationwide are chronically absent, missing more than 10 percent or more of the school year (*Albuquerque Journal,* September 10, 2013, p. B4).

- Children who are chronically absent have much lower reading scores than those who attend classes regularly (*Albuquerque Journal,* September 10, 2013, p. B4).

- High school dropouts have 60 percent more absences in first grade than high school graduates (*Albuquerque Journal,* September 10, 2013, p. B4).

- Research has shown that truancy is related to delinquency, substance use and abuse, high school dropout, suicidal thoughts and attempts, and early sexual intercourse (Chang and Romero 2008; Henry and Huizinga 2005, as reported in Heilbrunn 2007; Henry and Huizinga 2007; Kelley et al., 1997; Loeber and Farrington 2000; Seeley 2008a Truancy Prevention (www.ojjdp.gov/mpg/progTypesTruancy.aspx).

- Recent research shows that truancy is not only the most significant risk factor for predicting first-time marijuana use, but it also predicts 97 percent of first-time drug use (Seeley 2008).

- Decades of research have also identified a link between truancy and later problems in marriage, in jobs, and with violence, adult criminality, and incarceration (Dryfoos 1990; Catalano et al. 1998; Robins, and Ratcliff 1978; Snyder and Sickmund 1995).

- Truancy's high societal costs are evident in studies of adults who were frequent truants as adolescents. According to Baker, Sigmon, and Nugent (2001), such adults are more likely than others to:

  - have poor physical and mental health

  - work in low-paying jobs

- live in poverty
- utilize the welfare system extensively
- have children with problem behaviors
- be incarcerated.

(Source: www.ojjdp.gov/mpg/progTypesTruancy.aspx)

Suspension

- Black students are suspended more than three times as often as their white classmates, twice as often as their Latino classmates, and more than ten times as often as their Asian classmates in middle and high schools nationwide.

- The average American secondary student has an 11 percent chance of being suspended in a single school year, according to the study from the University of California–Los Angeles Civil Rights project. However, if that student is black, the odds of suspension jump to 24 percent. Reported by *USA Today*, May 12, 2013 (www.usatoday.com/story/news/nation/2013/05/12/black-student-suspensions/2151423/).

- Data from the US Department of Education's Office for Civil Rights found in 2006 that more than 28 percent of African-American middle school boys had been suspended at least once, compared with 10 percent of white males. For females, it was 18 percent of black students compared with 4 percent of white students. The Education Department found that 3.25 million students, or 7 percent of the total number of students in school, had been suspended at least once.

- A report designed by the director of the Justice Center at the Council of State Governments, a non-partisan group, found that 31 percent of Texas students were suspended off campus or expelled at least once during their years in middle and high school—at an average of almost four times apiece.

- About 15 percent were suspended or expelled at least eleven times, and nearly half of those ended up in the juvenile justice system. Most students who experience multiple suspensions or expulsions do not graduate, according to the study by the Council of State Governments Justice Center and the Public Policy Research Institute of Texas A&M University.

- In New Orleans, suspension rates have more than doubled over the last three decades across all grade levels. At the same time, racial gaps have widened: black students are three and a half times as likely to be suspended or expelled as their white peers.

- The Office for Civil Rights gathered the data from 72,000 schools in 7,000 districts, which educate approximately 85 percent of the country's students. The survey found one in five African-American males received an out-of-school suspension during the 2009–2010 academic year, compared to about one in fourteen white males.

- In the San Antonio Independent School District, special-education students were most disproportionately disciplined—16 percent received in-school suspension versus about 10 percent for the total student body. Disciplinary data for 2009–2010 collected by the Texas Education Agency show that African-American students, special-education students, and at-risk students are disciplined at higher rates.

- The most recent data from the National Center on Educational Statistics (NCES) showed that more than 3.3 million students were either suspended or expelled in 2006—nearly one in fourteen. Of these, fewer than one in ten were for offenses such as tardiness, talking back to a teacher, or violating a school's dress codes. For minority students, in 2006, about 15 percent of black students were suspended as compared with 7 percent of Hispanic students and 5 percent of white students.

In New York City, the Civil Liberties Union revealed that suspensions of 4-to-10-year-olds had increased 76 percent since 2003.

What Causes Truancy?

"Truancy" is defined as an unexcused absence from school, and it also applies to students who are chronically late. During 2007 and 2008, 30 percent of middle school students were chronically absent and 20 percent of elementary school students missed at least one month of school (according to H. Kim and J.J. Bathelemy, 2010, "A Tool for Assessing Truancy Risk among School Children: Predictive and Contract Validity of the Risk Indicator Survey," *Journal of Social Service Research,* 37(1): 50–60, www.tandfonline.com/doi/abs/10.1080/01488376.2011.524515?journalCode=wssr20#preview).

- **Home:** Several factors in a child's home or personal life can contribute to truancy. For example, if drugs or alcohol are used in the home, then children are at an increased risk of being absent from school. Other problems such as divorce, physical or verbal abuse, and frequent moving from place to place also cause chronic absenteeism. According to "Truancy as a Contextual and School-Related Problem: A Comparative Multilevel Analysis of Country and School Characteristics on Civic Knowledge among Fourteen Year Olds," children from lower income families are more vulnerable to truancy when compared to higher income families and parents who are not involved in their child's school life (E. Claes et al., 2009, "Truancy as a Contextual and School-Related Problem," *Educational Studies* 35(2): 123–142).

- **School:** A hostile school environment can also cause truancy. Students who lack friends or are being bullied are likely to skip school. This factor is especially applicable to students who look, act, or dress differently. In addition, some kids may face peer pressure to skip class. Truancy is seen among students who lack confidence in their mental abilities or have learning disabilities. High truancy rates are seen in schools that have antagonistic relationships between staff and students and a poor attendance policy.

- **Academic performance:** Being absent from class decreases a student's ability to learn. It is difficult to succeed if a student misses too much work, because it is hard to catch up. In addition, absent students lose interest in school, which results in low academic performance. Although truancy has known effects on individuals, truancy has negative effects on the overall learning environment.

- **Delinquency:** Without proper supervision during the day, truant teens are more likely to get involved in criminal activities, such as vandalism or shoplifting. Truancy can also lead to delinquency if students begin to associate with gangs. Being chronically absent from school causes children to engage in substance abuse. In fact, truancy is a risk factor for marijuana use.

Truancy is a warning sign for parents and educators. It indicates a lack of attachment to the school. Truancy is a sign of current trouble and an indicator of trouble to come.

What Schools Can Do to Deal with Truancy

The causes of truancy vary by age of students, ethnicity, economic status, geography, and other factors. Therefore each school and each community need to decide which steps to take to reduce truancy. These decisions should be made with the active involvement of parents, educators, law enforcement personnel, juvenile and family court judges, and representatives from social service, community, and religious organizations.

Truancy is expensive. It begins in elementary school and expands in middle school until the problem becomes catastrophic in high school. Schools lose funding because of excessive absences. Truants undermine mandates to raise standardized test scores. Truancy adds to a teacher's burden by forcing them to divert attention to bringing truant students back up to speed. Students become habitual absentees, losing instruction, being held back, and, ultimately, dropping out. Students who are not in school find things to do to occupy their time. Some drink, take drugs, get involved with other truant students, and commit crimes. It is in everyone's best interest to prevent habitual truancy.

The communities that have had the most success in deterring truancy have not only focused on improving procedures—such as those that accurately track student attendance—but have also implemented a comprehensive strategy that focuses on incentives and sanctions for truants and their parents. The following are nine primary elements of a comprehensive community and educational strategy to combat truancy.

1 Involve Parents in All Truancy Prevention Activities

Parents play the fundamental role in the education of their children. This applies to every family regardless of the parents' station in life, their income, or their educational background. Nobody else commands greater influence in getting a young person to go to school every day and to recognize how a good education can define his or her future.

For families and schools to work together to solve problems like truancy, there must be mutual trust and communication. Many truancy programs contain components that provide intensive monitoring, counseling, and other family-strengthening services to truants and their families. Schools can help by being "family-friendly" and encouraging teachers and parents to make regular contact before problems arise. Schools may want to consider arranging convenient times and neutral settings for parent meetings, starting homework hotlines, training teachers to work with parents, hiring or appointing a parent liaison, and giving parents a voice in school decisions.

Sometimes parents are complicit and enablers in their child's truancy. They provide reasons for them. Here are some excuses parents give for not sending their child to school:

- There was something more important to do.
- They needed to visit relatives (at home or in hospital) or relatives were coming to visit.
- There were family problems, emergencies.
- It was the child's/a family/someone's birthday.
- They needed to keep their mother company or help her.
- They were allowed to stay at home because they were tired.
- There were transportation difficulties.
- The weather was bad.
- It was Monday or Friday.
- They had problems with teachers.
- Bullying.
- There had been arguments between parents.
- It was a reward or punishment.

Schools need to be aware of these issues and take steps to avoid children and their parents from using these excuses.

2 Ensure That Students Face Firm Sanctions for Truancy

School districts should communicate to their students and their parents that they have zero tolerance for truancy. State legislatures have found that linking truancy to such items as a student's grades or driver's license can help reduce the problem. Delaware, Connecticut, and several other states have daytime curfews during school hours that allow law enforcement officers to question youth to determine if their absence is legitimate. In a few states, including New York, a student with a certain number of unexcused absences can be failed in his or her courses. A Wisconsin judge may, among other options, order a truant to attend counseling or to attend an education program designed for him or her.

3 Create Meaningful Incentives for Parental Responsibility

It is critical that parents of truant children assume responsibility for truant behavior. It is up to each community to determine the best way to create meaningful incentives for such parents to ensure that their children go to school. In some states, parents of truant children are asked to participate in parenting education programs. Some other states, such as Maryland and Oklahoma, have determined that parents who fail to prevent truancy can be subject to formal sanction or lose eligibility for certain public assistance. Communities can also provide positive incentives for responsible parents who ensure their child's regular school attendance. Such incentives can include increased eligibility to participate in publicly funded programs. Local officials, educators, and parents, working together, can make a shared commitment to assume responsibility for reducing truancy—and can choose the incentives that make the most sense for their community.

4 Establish Ongoing Truancy Prevention Programs in School

Truancy can be caused by or related to such factors as student drug use, violence at or near school, association with truant friends, lack of family support for regular attendance, emotional or mental health problems, lack of a clear path to more education or work, or inability to keep pace with academic requirements. Schools should address the unique needs of each child and consider developing initiatives to combat the root causes of truancy, including tutoring programs, added security measures, drug prevention initiatives, mentorship efforts through community and religious groups, campaigns for involving parents in their children's school attendance, and referrals to social service agencies.

Some schools are demanding that children with three unexcused absences attend a four-hour Saturday school on alternative weekends to help students recoup some of the learning they missed and in order to recoup some of the money the district is losing due to student absences.

Schools should also find new ways to engage their students in learning, including such hands-on options as career academies, school-to-work opportunities, and community service. They should enlist the support of local business and community leaders to determine the best way to prevent and reduce truancy. For example, business and community leaders may lend support by volunteering space to house temporary detention centers, establishing community service projects that lead to after-school or weekend jobs, or developing software to track truants.

5 Involve Local Law Enforcement in Truancy Reduction Efforts

In order to enforce school attendance policies, school officials should establish close linkages with local police, probation officers, and juvenile and family court officials. Police Departments report favorably on community-run temporary detention centers where they can drop off truant youth rather than bring them to local police stations for time-consuming processing. When part of a comprehensive anti-truancy initiative, police sweeps of local hangouts in which truant youth are often found can prove dramatically effective.

6 Parent(s) May Be an Abuser of Drugs and/or Alcohol

If schools become aware of parent alcohol or drug abuse, then the school has a responsibility to take some action. There are a variety of escalating steps that schools can take. They can refer a parent to Alcoholics Anonymous or Al-Anon, or Marijuana or Narcotics Anonymous. If parents refuse to take that step, then schools can notify social or law enforcement agencies.

7 Parents May Lack the Resources to Send Their Child to School

Sometimes a family may not have the funds to buy clothes that would enable a child to come to school. A family may lack an alarm clock. A family may not have the means to transport a child to school if they missed the school bus. A child may have an illness and the family may not have the money to pay for doctors or dentists. Schools need to maintain a list of resources in their community that can supply clothing, food, and health services.

8 Use Fellow Students to Reach Out

Some schools, especially in the lower grades, have had students in their classes write letters to absent students letting them know that they were missed.

9 Use Data to Measure Truancy

Schools should develop a variety of ways to track pupils and analyze attendance figures. Some suggested techniques include electronic registration and attendance systems, truancy sweeps, and observing substitute teachers. Since the causes of truancy are complex, the problem is unlikely to be resolved by a single approach. Therefore, early detection and intervention should help to prevent pupils from developing the habit.

(Source: US Department of Education in cooperation with the US Department of Justice)

What Parents Can Do to Prevent Truancy

- Ask the school to notify you when your child is absent. The school must notify you whether the absence is excused or unexcused, to ensure the child is not forging his own excuses.

- Investigate the safety of the child's school. An environment with gang or bullying issues encourages truancy.

- Explore alternative schools in your district. Other truant students can negatively influence your child and you may need to switch schools for severe problems. Talk to your school's guidance counselor about this possibility.

- Escort your child to school, either by walking with or driving the child. You can shield your child from violence or truant peers by taking them directly to their first class.

- Work with your child on subjects with which s/he struggles. Children skip school to avoid facing embarrassment in the classroom when their academic performance is poor.

- Make school a priority. Students must not miss school to help with the family business or to attend vacations that fall during the school year. Allowing students to miss school for reasons other than illness or family emergencies sends the message that school is not important.

- All LEAs (Local Education Authorities) and teachers believed that attendance is important because it is related to attainment, disruptive behavior, and children's safety.

- Several LEAs thought that schools are too ready to accept the reasons given for absence and also authorized too many absences because they were under pressure to reduce unauthorized absence.

- Most parents thought it was very important for children to attend school regularly. They associated regular attendance with children doing well in schoolwork.

- Parents perceived the main cause of truancy to be bullying, problems with teachers, and peer pressure to stay away from school.

- Parents of children with attendance problems perceived regular school attendance to be less important than parents of children who did not have attendance problems.

- Twenty-seven percent of primary school children said they had truanted without the collusion of their parents. This creates a cycle of poor attendance, which is hard to break. In 17 percent of these cases, the child was able to leave school without being detected.

- Many truants said the reason they wanted to miss school was boredom, and over half said they were not sorry afterwards. Most truants believed their parents would be angry to discover they had truanted.

- Sixteen percent of secondary school pupils admitted to truanting from school. White girls in Years 7, 8, and 9 (Grades 6–8) in all-white secondary schools are more likely to truant than boys, but less likely to truant than white boys in Years 7 and 8 in schools with a mixed racial intake. Very few secondary pupils from ethnic minority groups admitted to truancy.

- Secondary school pupils are more likely to attribute their absence from school to school-related factors than home-related factors. These reasons included problems with lessons, problems with teachers, being bullied, peer pressure, and social isolation.

- Most LEA representatives and teachers thought that truants had parents who placed a low value on education and were more likely to condone absence.

- Most primary teachers believed absence from school was always parentally condoned. Only a small number of primary school staff believed that school factors contributed to primary school children's absences.

- LEAs supported schools and promoted work with parents, general awareness raising amongst the general public and multi-agency work to combat truancy.

- Schools promoted good attendance through reward schemes, improvements to school ethos and facilities, closer links between primary and secondary schools, and building good relationships with parents.

- Nearly all schools used electronic registration systems to track pupils and analyze attendance figures. Some undertook truancy sweeps. Despite these systems determined pupils continued to skip classes, especially when being taught by substitute teachers.

- The causes of truancy are complex. Respondents identified a combination of home, school, and individual factors that cause some pupils to skip school. The problem is unlikely to be resolved by a single approach.

- Truancy starts young. Many pupils begin truanting in primary school and continue to do so in secondary school. Therefore, early intervention would be worthwhile to prevent pupils developing the habit.

- Truancy is an unrecognized problem. Although boys are more likely than girls to truant in primary school, the position is reversed in grades 7, 8 and 9 in all-white secondary schools. Further research is required into how girls and their families can be supported.

- The causes of truancy are contested. Parents and pupils stress school-related factors as the main cause of truancy, but LEAs and teachers believe that parental attitudes and home environments are more influential.

- Truancy causes harm. Most harm is done to the truants themselves, who are a minority of the school population. The effects on other pupils and teachers varied, but returning truants disrupt the learning of other pupils, divert the teachers' attention, and frustrate and demoralize teachers.

- Truancy is costly. Despite the fact that only a small proportion of pupils are regular truants, LEAs, teachers, and other professionals spend a disproportionate amount of time encouraging good attendance and dealing with poor attendance. Schools lose funding when students do not attend. The value for money of these measures needs exploring.

- Distinguishing authorized/unauthorized absence is unhelpful because schools apply the terms in different ways. In addition, the classification masks the scale of the problem faced by schools and focuses teachers' attention on ways of presenting the statistics rather than seeking solutions to the attendance problem.

- A variety of strategies are employed. LEAs and schools employ a variety of strategies to encourage good attendance and deal with poor attendance. These include electronic registration systems, truancy sweeps, and contact with parents and support for pupils with poor attendance. However, the efficacy of each has not been established.

- Multi-agency working is advocated. LEAs and schools have begun to work with other agencies in order to address the complexity of truancy. There are, however, tensions inherent in multi-agency working because each agency has its own priorities.

- Schools need to change. Many persistent truants reported that they were bored with school. In addition, they were more easily able to truant when taught by substitute teachers. A stronger focus on retaining staff, cutting down on staff absences, developing appropriate curricula, teaching styles and school ethos is needed. Very persistent truants might benefit from alternatives to school.

- Sometimes parents unknowingly contribute to their child's truancy by providing excuses as to why children do not attend school. These should not be used as a wedge between their child and the school.

(Source: H. Malcolm et al., 2003, *Absence from School: A Study of Its Causes and Effects in Seven LEAs*, Glasgow: SCRE Centre, University of Glasgow)

Tasks to Be Done While in In-School Suspension

In order to cut down on out-of-school suspensions, which can result in student failure and the possibility of them dropping out, schools have been using in-school suspension as an alternative.

Children who are placed in in-school suspension should not perceive it to be "a badge of courage." They need to recognize that they did something wrong. The assignment in Box 9.1 could be the first task they are asked to complete. Some students who are placed in in-school suspension programs deny any responsibility about why they have been placed in in-school suspension rooms. The following exercise can be used to have them explain their side of the story. Their answers can also be sent to their parents.

Box 9.1 *Tasks to Be Done While in In-School Suspension*

Directions: For the following questions, answer each to the best of your ability. Each answer **must** be three paragraphs (five complete sentences) in length. Use correct capitalization and punctuation in each answer! Answer each question with as much detail as possible.

1 What were the events leading up to you being placed in in-school suspension?

2 Why did this happen?

3 How do you feel about being placed in in-school suspension?

4 What can you do in the future, to problem solve appropriately, so that you will not be placed in in-school suspension?

5 To whom should you apologize? Write out that apology.

Youth Gambling

Gambling has become so engrained in the American landscape that it has become transparent—invisible. Legalized gambling is a socially acceptable, widely promoted activity. In the past, gambling was recognized as an adult pastime. In recent years, it has increased significantly among young people who have grown up in a society where it is legal and widely accepted. Movies, television shows, the widespread casino movement, and increased access to gaming through the Internet have increased the availability of gambling. States run legal lotteries. Casinos exist in most states. Las Vegas and Atlantic City have become destination cities. Gambling on sporting events is an accepted part of sports. Internet gambling brings in almost $30 billion annually (www.americangaming.org/sites/default/files/uploads/docs/final_online_gambling_white_paper_5-18-11.pdf).

As a result, many young people under the age of 18 are gambling. Many problem youth gamblers say they started out at approximately 10 years of age. Lacking many outward signs of addiction (needle marks, drowsy walking, bloodshot eyes), youth gambling is easy to hide.

Schools, as part of society, reflect the American passion for gambling. While much of the gambling taking place in schools is harmless, it occasionally lays the foundation for compulsive and habitual gambling. Students play cards in the lunchroom or study halls, they play dice in the bathrooms or in the schoolyard, and educators either don't see it or ignore it.

While much of youth gambling takes place off school grounds, school environments are conducive to gambling behaviors through permissiveness or lack of awareness. Are students playing card games (for money) during lunch period or study halls? Is there betting on high school basketball or football games? Do students bet on "March Madness"? Young people need to understand that gambling is not risk free. Research has shown that gambling, like other addictions, has "risk factors" and can increase a person's susceptibility to an addiction. Many of the gambling studies conducted with young people and problem gambling show that the younger an individual is when they start, the more at risk they are of developing a gambling problem as adults. Youth gambling activities include sports betting, poker, other card games, crane games, dice, board games, pitching quarters, lottery, pull tabs, and Internet gambling,

Schools are impacted because some of these students become so addicted that they go into debt, stealing money from parents and families or "shaking down" fellow students to get more money in order to gamble.

Background

According to the National Council of Problem Gambling:

- Teen rates for problem gambling are higher than for adults. Young adults between the ages of 18 and 24 were found to have problem gambling rates that doubled those of older adults (www.choosehelp. com/gambling-addiction/teen-gambling-and-teen-problem-gambling/ teenage-gambling-2013-how-big-is-the-problem).

- Almost three-quarters of teens admit to gambling within the last twelve months (www.choosehelp.com/gambling-addiction/teen-gambling-and-teen-problem-gambling/teenage-gambling-2013-how-big-is-the-problem).

- Approximately 4–8 percent of children between 12 and 17 years of age meet the criteria for a gambling problem, and another 10–15 percent are at risk of developing a problem.

- Teenagers' preferred games include free Internet gambling, card games, and sports bets. One young person per classroom already has a hidden gambling problem (R.A. Volberg et al., 2010, "An International Perspective on Youth Gambling Prevalence Studies," *International Juvenile Adolescence Medical Health* 22(1): 3–38, http://tinyurl.com/qjqlcws).

- Canadian studies of students in the 7th through 11th grades have indicated that approximately 87 percent have gambled (for money) at least once in their lifetime. 47.1 percent of 7th grade children have purchased lottery tickets between six and nineteen times in one month (R. Gupta and J. L. Derevensky, 1998, "Adolescent Gambling Behavior: A Prevalence Study and Examination of the Correlates Associated with Problem Gambling," *Journal of Gambling Studies* 14(4): 319–345).

Teen problem gamblers have higher rates of:

- alcohol and binge drinking (Student Wellness Survey 2012, www. oregon.gov/oha/amh/pages/student-wellness/index.aspx)
- drug use (Student Wellness Survey 2012)
- suicidal thoughts and attempts (Student Wellness Survey 2012)
- school problems (e.g., lower grades, truancy, and behavior issues) (Student Wellness Survey 2012)
- violent behavior (Oregon Healthy Teens 2009, http://problemgamling prevention.org/curricula/hs/hs-health-teen-gambling-awareness-hklb-pgs.pdf)
- family problems (e.g., withdrawal, behavior issues)
- risky sexual behavior (Oregon Healthy Teens 2009)
- peer relationship problems
- legal and money troubles
- depression
- dissociative, "escape" behaviors
- risk for other addictions including alcohol and substance abuse.

Risk factors include:

- an early "big win"
- family history of problem gambling, or substance abuse
- loneliness or boredom
- peer pressure
- low self-esteem
- poor coping skills
- a lack of identity and purpose in life.

What Schools Can Do to Decrease the Risks of Problem Gambling

- Include gambling awareness information in curricula or in guidance classes. There are a number of gambling awareness curricula that can be used to provide training:

  - www.problemgamblingprevention.org/curricula/hs/hs-health-teen-gambling-awareness-hklb-pgs.pdf

  - www.1877mylimit.org/modelschoolprogram.asp

  - www.ncrg.org/public-education-and-outreach/college-and-youth-gambling-programs/talking-children-about-gambling

  - Youth Gambling Resources, https://portfolio.du.edu/portfolio/getportfoliofile?uid=55753.

- School personnel should have an awareness of the signs of gambling. These include:

  - unexplained absences from school

  - school grades dropping

  - increased family conflict

  - the family suspects alcohol or other drug abuse

  - asking/taking/stealing money from family and/or friends

  - large amounts of money in youth's possession

  - gambling language and gambling an important conversational topic

  - showing off money, clothing, and other possessions

  - spending an unusual amount of time on the computer

  - reading periodicals to do with sports or online betting sites

  - selling personal belongings

  - bragging about winnings

  - exhaustion from lack of sleep.

- Provide training through professional development programs for teachers, administrators, and counselors.

- Train student assistance teams and school mental health personnel to assess for problem gambling and refer students to appropriate treatment resources.

- Review or establish a school policy on gambling and promote enforcement of the policy.

(Source: Connecticut Council on Problem Gambling)

Box 10.1 *A Gambling Self-Test*

Student gambling is just as addictive as adult gambling but many students do not recognize it as a problem. This test may create awareness in your students.

The following questions may help you explore how gambling is affecting your life.

- Do you often find yourself thinking about gambling activities and/or planning the next time you will play?

- Do you need to spend more and more money on gambling activities to get the same level of excitement?

- Do you become restless, tense, fed up, or bad-tempered when trying to cut down or stop gambling?

- Do you ever gamble to escape or forget problems?

- After losing money on gambling activities, do you ever return another day to try and win your money back?

- Have you lied to your family and friends about your gambling?

- Have you spent your lunch or transportation money on gambling activities?

- Have you taken money from someone you live with, without his or her knowledge, in order to gamble?

- Have you stolen money from outside the family or shoplifted in order to gamble?

- Have you experienced problems with members of your family or close friends because of your gambling?

- Have you missed school or work in order to participate in gambling activities?

- Have you ever had to ask for help because of your gambling?

- Is gambling the most exciting activity in your life?

- Do you try to prevent your family and friends from knowing how much or how often you gamble?

- Do you miss school, work, activities, or other events due to gambling?

- Has anyone expressed concern about your gambling?

- Do you lie to your friends or family about your gambling? For example, do you ever tell people that you did not gamble or that you won money gambling when you really lost money or possessions?

- Do you borrow money to gamble?

- Have you sold personal belongings to get money to gamble?

- Do you often gamble with money you intended to use for other things (lunch, clothing, CDs, etc.)?

- Have you stolen from your family, friends, or employer to gamble or pay gambling debts?

- After losing, do you try to win your money back by gambling?

- Do you often find yourself thinking about gambling activities and/or planning the next time you will play?

- Do you get into arguments with your parents because of gambling or with your friends over a gambling activity?

- Do you feel depressed or lose sleep or feel guilty because you lost money gambling?

- Do you ever gamble to escape or forget problems?

- Do you become restless, tense, fed-up, or bad-tempered when trying to cut down on your gambling?

- Have you tried to stop gambling but can't?

If you answered "yes" to some of these questions, you may have a gambling problem. Speak to a Guidance Counselor, your parents or a trusted teacher.

(Source: A Self-test for Teens: from the Arizona Office of Problem Gambling; International Centre for Youth Gambling and High-Risk Behaviors, McGill University)

Six Things Parents Can Do to Decrease the Risks of Problem Gambling

1   Learn the facts about gambling in your state: age restrictions, types of gambling, and gambling terminology.

2   Examine your own attitudes about gambling and provide positive role models.

3   Know the warning signs of problem gambling and be alert to changes in behavior that might indicate that your child has a problem.

4   Talk to your children about the risks associated with gambling.

5   Parents have the ability to influence their child's behavior by providing open areas of communication if they believe their child has become a habitual gambler, and by teaching children about the risks and consequences of gambling.

6   Encourage schools and other organizations involved with young people to distribute information on the risks associated with gambling.

(Source: Connecticut Council on Problem Gambling)

11 Conclusion

Violence exists in the world in which today's children live. They see it every day. There is violence in newspapers, on television, in electronic video games. Many live in violent neighborhoods. Increased violence in their home includes familial violence and physical, emotional, and sexual abuse. It thrives in sports, whether wrestling or football. Bullying flourishes in politics and in families. Young children see sexual situations on soap operas and in PG-rated movies. While most children do not dramatize these situations, some do. They take advantage of others in their homes, in the street, and in school.

One need only look at the local evening television news to see examples of the mayhem that has taken place during the day (murders, shooting, rapes, child abuse, etc.). Societal violence bleeds into schools. And since schools reflect society, its values, and its cultures, schools reflect this violence.

According to the Center to Prevent Handgun Violence, for every household in the US, private citizens own two guns. The FBI estimates that there are 200 million privately owned firearms. That equals ninety guns for every hundred people. In 2011 there were 34,000 gun deaths in America. In that same year there were 1,000 gun deaths in Chicago (population 2,695,598) and forty-five in London (population 7,556,900). It is not surprising that some of these guns fall into the hands of young people. According to the US Department of Education's latest report on the Gun-Free Schools Act (www2.ed.gov/about/reports/annual/gfsa/gfsarptrev ised4413.pdf), there was a 10 percent increase in the number of guns found on students from 2008–2009 to the 2010–2011 school year. In Washington, DC, which has one of the nation's toughest anti-handgun laws, young people can easily buy guns on the black market. Or they can even "rent" a weapon for a short time. Ten people were killed and forty-two others were wounded in shootings over the 2012 Memorial Day weekend in Chicago. The increase in gang activity and drug trafficking also contribute to the escalation in violence. Many students in crime-ridden inner-city areas carry weapons for "protection" from robberies and gang fights. If the number of guns is reduced in American society, I have no doubt that the number of school-related incidents of gun violence would also diminish. That does not mean that schools can avoid dealing with the problem. Because schools are a part of society, they merely reflect society. But before schools can become citadels of learning they must become sanctuaries of safety.

Are American schools less violent or more violent than in the past? Students today stand less of a chance of dying violently in school than a century ago. What has dramatically changed is that school violence is far more visible due to the exploitive nature of television, including the news, the movies, video games, smart phones, and YouTube. When governors cut school budgets, resulting in lowering the number of adults in schools, and increase class sizes, they are putting students in closer proximity to one another with fewer visible adults; this will increase the likelihood of school fights and other school violence.

School violence is the inevitable result of bringing large numbers of culturally and ethnically diverse people together in a confined space. Doing so increases the possibility of violence. But schools can take steps to improve plans for preventing and responding to crises and ensuring supports are in place to foster the recovery of those affected. Schools alone cannot fix all the drama and trauma in children's lives, but they should at least be a safe haven for children and staff. In our changing society, students bring their problems into schools, and schools need to address these problems before instruction can take place.

The real question that needs to be answered is: How serious is America about protecting its children and public education? Children, parents, and educators want, need, and deserve a safe, secure, predictable, stable environment in which to learn. Parents have a right to expect that when their children leave for school in the morning they will return home at the end of the day. Children need adults whom they can trust, who have been properly trained, and who are prepared to respond to the issue of school violence. Unless, and until, society is prepared to deal with these challenges, America needs to be prepared for increased school violence.

This book has broadly defined violence in and around schools. Keeping schools safe is not, and should not be, merely about preventing school violence. Thankfully, most schools will not see gun violence or suicides. However, staff, parents, and students should be prepared to deal with all aspects of school violence including bullying, alcohol and drug use, youth gambling, sexuality, and Internet safety. Schools need to prepare for any eventuality, including the possibility of violence. Being prepared is about the school organization, the school infrastructure, and individuals. Have safety checks been performed, and are all staff members aware of what their roles and responsibilities are in dealing with students who demonstrate possible signs of violence to others or to themselves?

Joe Bergant, Superintendent of the Chardon Local Schools, in Chardon, Ohio, where five students were shot, resulting in three deaths, stated, "This could happen anywhere." At the same time, it is important to realize that fifty-five million children went to school on the day that twenty were massacred at Sandy Hook Elementary School in Newton, Connecticut. The chances of a child dying in a school shooting are remote. Seventy mass shootings have occurred in the US since 1982, leaving 543 dead. While this is tragic, schools are still safer than the streets and even still safer than students' homes.

Answers to the Violence Prevention Quiz

1   *Blackboard Jungle* was a 1955 film about teachers in an inner-city school. It is based on the novel of the same name by Evan Hunter. The film starred Glenn Ford as a teacher at North Manual High School, an inner-city school where many of the pupils, led by student Sidney Poitier, frequently engaged in school violence. The point is that school violence is not a new phenomenon but has left the inner city and moved to the suburban and rural areas. The nature of the violence has also changed and now affects white, frequently affluent students.

2   Knives, box cutters, and razor blades.

3   Beer or prescription drugs. Both of them are inexpensive. Increasingly students are stealing their parents' pills and having pill parties. A pill party is one in which people bring all different kinds of over-the-counter and prescription medications. It usually involves mixing all these pills together and placing them into shot glasses or other cups and taking them at once. It can lead to a high or altered fantasy state depending on the drug interactions and the body's response, or it can lead to liver failure, heart and lung issues, and death if you are very unlucky in the pill mix that is ingested. Hard-core drug users also mix designer drugs. They may be used in high school and early college age groups.

4   Our Lady of Angels School fire occurred in Chicago, December 1, 1958, resulting in the deaths of ninety-two students and three teachers (who were nuns). A boy age 10, who was a 5th grader, confessed. He took and passed a lie detector test.

5   Schools are safer. The number of violent deaths on school grounds declined to thirty-three in the 2009–2010 school year, the lowest

number on record since the US Departments of Education and Justice began collecting data in 1992. In the previous school year, there were thirty-eight such deaths. Thefts and non-fatal violent crimes declined from 1.2 million in 2008 to 828,00 in 2010. The highest number of violent school deaths—sixty-three–occurred in the 2006–2007 school year. While the data show a consistent decline in violent deaths, there were increases in cyberbullying and suicides among youths aged 5–18 outside of school. Of the thirty-three violent deaths involving students, staff members, and others on campuses, twenty-five were homicides, five were suicides, and three involved a law enforcement officer.

6 Homicide. According to the Centers for Disease Control and Prevention (CDC; A. M. Miniño, 2010, "NCHS Data Brief No. 37 Mortality Among Teenagers Aged 12–19 Years: United States, 1999–2006," www.cdc.gov/nchs/data/databriefs/db37.htm), 45.3 percent of black male deaths between the ages of 15 and 19 are caused by homicide.

7 161,000. They are afraid of being bullied or attacked.

8 Nothing. Although almost all of them were male. Only two female school shooting incidents have been documented.

9 There is no credible evidence that zero tolerance reduces violence or drug abuse by students (according to R. J. Skiba, 2000, "Zero Tolerance, Zero Evidence: An Analysis of School Disciplinary Practice," Policy Research Report #SRS2 and APA Zero Tolerance Task Force, 2008, "Are Zero Tolerance Policies Effective in the Schools? An Evidentiary Review and Recommendations," *American Psychologist,* www.apa.org/pubs/info/reports/zero-tolerance.pdf).

10 Less than 1 percent. Schools are one of the safest places for children to be.

11 According to the US Department of Education, most bullying takes place in middle schools.

12 False. Females are more likely to bully than males.

13 Most school violence occurs in middle schools.

14 False. Although sexual abuse by educators garners media headlines, data indicate that most sexual abuse is inter-familial.

15 True. According to the Office of Juvenile Justice, 70 percent of the students who bring guns to school do so to protect themselves from bullies or gangs. However, by bringing a gun to school they not only

violate the law, they must also be expelled if caught, and they may use the weapon.

16 According to a report from the Archives of Pediatric and Adolescent Medicine, more than a quarter of American teenagers have sent nude pictures of themselves ("sexting").

17 According to the FBI, there are between 200–300 million guns in the United States, or about two guns for every person. Some of these guns make their way into schools.

18 According to the CDC, two-thirds of teens and young adults have had oral sex—about as many as have had vaginal intercourse. The research shows that one in four teens is now having oral sex before vaginal sex.

19 The Office of Juvenile Justice reports that most gangs exist in urban areas but there has been a dramatic increase in gangs in rural and sub-urban areas.

20 False. The same report indicates that females are becoming increasingly violent, even committing murder.

Additional Resources

I wish to thank the many fine individuals and those from State Departments of Education, who have done marvelous research or have generously posted their material on the Internet and given me permission to use their material.

I have used well over 250 different sources to obtain information and research dealing with each topic. There is a plethora of information for those who seek it. Other than the sources listed on the pages of the book, the ones that follow are the ones I have found to be the most helpful, accurate, and kept up to date. The best of the best are the Centers for Disease Control and Prevention (CDC; www.cdc.gov), the Office of Juvenile Justice and Delinquency Prevention (OJJDP) of the US Department of Justice (www.ojjdp.gov), the National Institutes of Health (www.nih.gov/), and the National Center for Educational Statistics (NCES) (nces.ed.gov/).

As a result of the shootings at Columbine High School in Colorado, the FBI (M. E. O'Toole, n.d., "The School Shooter Report: A Threat Assessment Perspective," www.fbi.gov/stats-services/publications/school-shooter) and the Secret Service (R. A. Fein et al., *Threat Assessment in Schools: A Guide to Managing Threatening Situations and to Creating Safe School Climates*, Washington, DC: US Secret Service and US Department of Education, www.secretservice.gov/ntac/ssi_guide.pdf) interviewed all of the surviving perpetrators and victims and issued two reports. Readers can and should download them.

The following are excellent sources and were current when accessed:

Abma, J. C., Martinez, G. M., Mosher, W. D. and Dawson, B. S. (2002). "Teenagers in the United States: Sexual Activity, Contraceptive Use, and Childbearing." *Vital Health Statistics* 23(24): 1–48.

Alan Guttmacher Institute (2004). *U.S. Teenage Pregnancy Statistics: Overall Trends, Trends by Race and Ethnicity and State-by state Information.* New York: Alan Guttmacher Institute.

Barr, R. and Parrett, W. (2001). *Hope Fulfilled for At-risk and Violent Youth: K–12 Programs that Work.* Needham Height, MA: Allyn and Bacon.

Beane, A. (2011). *The New Bully Free Classroom: Proven Prevention and Intervention Strategies for Teachers K–8.* Minneapolis, MN: Free Spirit Publishing.

Bleakley, A. and Ellis, J.A. (2003). "A Role for Health Research in Shaping Adolescent Health Policy." *American Journal of Public Health* 93(11): 1801–1802.

Bureau of Justice Assistance (2009). *Guide for Preventing and Responding to School Violence,* 2nd edn. Washington, DC: Bureau of Justice Assistance, US Department of Justice. www.bja.gov/Publications/IACP_School_Violence.pdf.

Centers for Disease Control and Prevention (2003). "Trends in Reportable Sexually Transmitted Diseases in the United States," www.cdc.gov/STD/stats07/trends.htm.

Centers for Disease Control and Prevention (2004). *Youth Risk Behavior Surveillance—United States, 2003.* Surveillance Summaries, MMWR 2004: 53 (No.SS-2). www.cdc.gov/mmwr/pdf/ss/ss5302.pdf.

Centers for Disease Control and Prevention (2004). *Sexually Transmitted Disease Surveillance 2004.* Atlanta, GA: US Department of Health and Human Services. www.cdc.gov/std/stats04/2004SurveillanceAll.pdf.

Chambliss, W. (ed.). (2011). *Crime and Criminal Behavior.* Thousand Oaks, CA: Sage.

Cullen, D. (2009). *Columbine.* New York: Grand Central Publishing.

Cushman, K. and Delpit, L. (2005). *Fires in the Bathroom: Advice for Teachers from High School Students.* New York: New Press.

Cushman, K. and Rogers, L. (2009). *Fires in the Middle School Bathroom: Advice for Teachers from Middle Schoolers.* New York: New Press.

Darroch, J.E., Singh, S., and Frost, J.J. (2001). "Differences in Teenage Pregnancy Rates among Five Developed Countries: The Roles of Sexual Activity and Contraceptive Use." *Family Planning Perspectives* 33: 244–250, 281.

Drew, N. (2010). *No Kidding About Bullying: 125 Ready-to-Use Activities to Help Kids Manage Anger, Resolve Conflicts, Build Empathy, and Get Along (Bully Free Classroom)*. Minneapolis, MN: Free Spirit Publishing.

Griffith, M., Lee, W., and Yang, W. (2003). *Healthy People Nevada 2010*. Carson City, NV: Center for Health and Data Research.

Hanel, C. and Trolley, L. S. B. (2010). *Browser the Mouse and his Internet Adventure*. Thousand Oaks, CA: Corwin Press.

Henshaw, S. K. (2004). *U.S. Teenage Pregnancy Statistics with Comparative Statistics for Women Aged 20–24*. New York: Alan Guttmacher Institute.

Hindjuda, S. and Patchin, J.W. (2008). *Bullying beyond the Schoolyard: Preventing and Responding to Cyberbullying*. Thousand Oaks, CA: Corwin Press.

Hindjuda, S. and Patchin, J.W. (2011). *Cyberbullying Prevention and Response: Expert Perspectives*. Thousand Oaks, CA: Corwin Press.

Jones, R. K., Darroch, J. E., and Henshaw, S. K. (2002). *Pattterns in the Socio-economic Characteristics of Women Obtaining Abortions in 2000–2001*. New York: Alan Guttmacher Institute.

Kenley, H. (2011). *Cyber Bullying No More: Parenting A High Tech Generation (Growing with Love)*. Ann Arbor, MI. Loving Healing Press.

Kozol, J. (1968). *Death at an Early Age*. New York: Bantam Books.

Larson, E. (1995). *Lethal Passage: The Story of a Gun*. New York: Vintage Books.

Martin, J. A., Hamilton, B. E., Sutton, P. D., et al., (2005). "Births: Final Data for 2003." *National Vital Statistics Reports* 54(2): 1–116.

Mosher, W. D., Chandra A., and Jones, J. (2005). *Sexual Behavior and Selected Health Measures: Men and Women 15–44 Years of Age, United States, 2002*. Advance Data from Vital and Health Statistics, No. 362. Hyattsville, MD: National Center for Health Statistics.

Myers, J., McCaw, D., and Hemphill, L. (2011). *Responding to Cyber Bullying: An Action Tool for School Leaders*. Thousand Oaks, CA: Corwin Press.

National Campaign to Prevent Teen Pregnancy. (2003). *Science Says: The Sexual Behavior of Young Adolescents?* Washington, DC: National Campaign to Prevent Teen Pregnancy.

National Campaign to Prevent Teen Pregnancy (2004). *Fact Sheet: How is the 34 Percent Statistic Calculated?* Washington, DC: National Campaign to Prevent Teen Pregnancy.

National Campaign to Prevent Teen Pregnancy (2004). *Sexual Attitudes and Behavior of Young Adolescents.* Washington, DC: National Campaign to Prevent Teen Pregnancy.

National Campaign to Prevent Teen Pregnancy (2004). *Teen Pregnancy—So What?* Washington, DC: National Campaign to Prevent Teen Pregnancy.

National Gang Center and Office of Juvenile Justice (2011). "A Parents' Guide to Gangs." www.nationalgangcenter.gov/Parents-Guide-to-Gangs.

Peck, S. W. (2012). *STAND TALL Teacher's Manual & DVD, Grades 4–6: Lessons that Teach Respect and Prevent Bullying.* Thousand Oaks, CA: Corwin Press.

Rea, D. and Bergin, J. (1999). *Safeguarding Our Youth: Successful School & Community Programs.* New York: McGraw-Hill Higher Education.

Robers, S., Kemp, J., and Truman, J. (2013). *Indicators of School Crime and Safety: 2012* (NCES 2013–036/NCJ 241446). Washington, DC: National Center for Education Statistics, US Department of Education, and Bureau of Justice Statistics, Office of Justice Programs, US Department of Justice.

Rogers, S. (2009). *My First Year in the Classroom.* Avon, MA: Adams Media.

Saferstein, R. (2009). *Forensic Science: From the Crime Scene to the Crime Lab.* Boston, MA: Pearson Education.

Saferstein, R. (2011). *Forensic Science: An Introduction.* Boston, MA: Pearson Education.

Schargel, F. P. (2003). *Dropout Prevention Tools.* Larchmont, NY: Routledge.

Schargel, F. P. (2005). *Best Practices to Help At-Risk Learners.* Larchmont, NY: Routledge.

Schargel, F. P (2008). *152 Ways to Keep Students in School: Effective, Easy-to-Implement Tips for Teachers.* Larchmont, NY: Routledge.

Schargel, F.P. (2011). *Dropout Prevention Fieldbook.* Larchmont, NY: Routledge.

Shariff, S. (2009). *Cyber-bullying: Issues and Solutions for the School, the Classroom and the Home.* Cambridge, UK: Cambridge University Press.

Singh, S. and Darroch, J. E. (2000). "Adolescent Pregnancy and Childbearing: Levels and Trends in Developed Countries." *Family Planning Perspectives* 32(1): 14–23.

Simmons, R. (2002). *Odd Girl Out: The Hidden Culture of Aggression in Girls.* New York: Mariner Books.

Smith, G. (2007). *Remembering Garrett: One Family's Battle with a Child's Depression.* New York: Basic Books.

Strickland, M. (2011). *More than a Test Score: Strategies for Empowering Youth at Risk.* Lanham, MA: Rowman and Littlefield Education.

Sullivan, K., Cleary, M., and Sullivan, G. (2004). *Bullying in the Secondary School: What it Looks Like and How to Manage It.* Thousand Oaks, CA: Corwin Press.

Thacker, T., Schargel, F., and Bell, J. (2009). *Creating School Cultures that Embrace Learning: What Successful Schools Do.* Larchmont, NY, Routledge.

US Department of Education, Office of Safe and Healthy Students (2013). *Report on the Implementation of the Gun Free Schools Act in the States and Outlying Areas for School Year 2010–11;* Washington, DC: US Department of Education, Office of Safe and Healthy Students.

Wrobleski, A. (1995). *Suicide: Why?: 85 Questions and Answers about Suicide.* New York: Afterwords Publications.

Wrobleski, A. (2002). *Suicide Survivors: A Guide for Those Left Behind.* New York: Afterwords Publications.

Bullying Websites

- Cyberbullying Research Center, www.cyberbullying.us/
- Common Sense Media, www.commonsensemedia.org/educators/cyberbullying-toolkit
- Ken Rigby.net, www.kenrigby.net/
- Teaching Tolerance, www.tolerance.org/
- A Thin Line, www.athinline.org
- National Office of Missing and Exploited Children, www.missingkids.com/
- NetSmartz, www.netsmartz.org
- Stay Safe Online, www.staysafeonline.org
- ChildrenOnline, http://childrenonline.org
- ConnectSafely, www.connectsafely.org
- FTC Net-Cetera, www.onguardonline.gov/topics/net-cetera.aspx
- GetParentalControls, http://getparentalcontrols.org
- Ryan's Story, www.ryanpatrickhalligan.org

- Hinduja and Patchin, http://cyberbullying.us/links.php
- Wired Safety, www.wiredsafety.org

Additional Bullying Resources in Spanish

The following are selected links, research, and resources for Spanish-speaking families. It is by no means an exhaustive list. All the resources are free to use. For some, print materials are also available.

- NetCetera/Spanish, www.alertaenlinea.gov
- http://kidshealth.org/parent/centers/spanish_center_esp.html

Gang Violence Websites

- "It's About Time: Prevention and Intervention Services for Gang-affiliated Girls," www.nccdglobal.org/sites/default/files/publication_pdf/focus-its-about-time.pdf
- Provides Anti-gang Training, www.nationalgangcenter.gov
- Gangs and School safety, www.schoolsecurity.org/trends/gangs.html
- Stop the Violence: Gang Prevention in Schools, www.stanford.edu/class/e297c/poverty_prejudice/ganginterv/stopvio.htm
- Gang Prevention, www.nasponline.org/resources/principals/nassp_gang.pdf
- GREAT, www.great-online.org/
- What Can You Do to Prevent Gang Violence, http://ganginfo.rlcw.org/youcan.htm
- National Youth Prevention Resource Center, www.nsvrc.org/organizations/87
- Office of Juvenile Justice's *Promising Strategies to Reduce Gun Violence*, www.ojjdp.gov/pubs/gun_violence/173950.pdf

Internet Safety Websites

- Rockingham County Internet Safety Pages, www.rockingham.k12.va.us/netsafety/netsafety-schools.htm

- Web Wise Kids, www.webwisekids.org
- Hector's World, http://hectorsworld.netsafe.org.nz
- ChildrenOnline, http://childrenonline.org
- ConnectSafely, www.connectsafely.org
- Family Online Safety Institute, www.fosi.org/cms
- FTC Net-Cetera, www.onguardonline.gov/topics/net-cetera.aspx
- GetParentalControls, http://getparentalcontrols.org
- Ryan's Story, www.ryanpatrickhalligan.org
- Cyberbullying Research Links Page, http://cyberbullying.us/links.php
- Net Family News, www.netfamilynews.org
- OSPI Safety Center, www.k12.wa.us/SafetyCenter
- *Enhancing Child Safety and Online Technologies,* http://cyber.law. harvard.edu/publications/2009/ISTTF_Final_Report
- SafeKids, www.safekids.com
- Wired Kids, http://wiredkids.org/
- Wired Safety, www.wiredsafety.org

Additional Internet Resources in Spanish

The following are selected links, research, and resources for Spanish-speaking families. It is by no means an exhaustive list. All the resources are free to use. For some, print materials are also available.

- FTC—NetCetera/Spanish, www.alertaenlinea.gov
- Kids Health/Spanish, http://kidshealth.org/parent/en_espanol/net_safety_ esp.html

Use of the Internet

- Online Safety Resources, Seattle Public Schools, www.seattleschools. org/area/policies/c/C23.00.pdf
- Anti-harassment/Cyber-bullying, www.seattleschools.org/area/policies/d/ D49.00.pdf

- Seattle School District Internet Use Forms, http://inside.seattleschools. org/area/dots/webinternet/NetworkUseAgreement_Student2009.pdf

- Staff Network Use Agreement, https://inside.seattleschools.org/area/ dots/forms/networkuseagreement.pdf

- Safe@school, www.safeatschool.ca/

Suicide Prevention

Suicide Support Groups and Organizations

American Academy of Child & Adolescent Psychiatry
3615 Wisconsin Ave., NW,
Washington, DC 20016-3007
Phone: 202/966-7300
Fax: 202/966-2891
Website: www.aacap.org

American Association of Suicidology
4201 Connecticut Ave., NW,
Suite 408
Washington, DC 20008
Phone: 202/237-2280
Fax: 202/237-2282
Website: www.suicidology.org

American Foundation for Suicide Prevention
120 Wall St., 22nd Floor
New York, NY 10005
Phone: 888/333-AFSP (2377) (toll-free)
212/363-3500
Fax: 212/363-6237
Website: www.afsp.org

SAVE (Suicide Awareness Voices of Education)
8120 Penn Ave. S, Suite 470
Bloomington, MN 55431
Phone: 952-946-7998
Website: www.save.org

SPAN-USA (Suicide Prevention Advocacy Network)
1025 Vermont Ave., NW, Suite 1066
Washington, DC 20005
Phone: 202-449-3600
Fax: 202-449-3601
Website: www.afsp.org/

Yellow Ribbon Suicide Prevention Program
P.O. Box 644
Westminster, CO 80030-0644
Phone: 303-429-3530
Fax: 303-426-4496
Website: www.yellowribbon.org

Suicide Prevention National Telephone Number

- National Crisis Line (800) 784-2433

Suicide Prevention Website Resources

- American Academy of Pediatrics, www.aap.org/advocacy/childhealth month/prevteensuicide.htm
- Teen Suicide, www.focusas.com/Suicide.html
- Teens Health, http://kidshealth.org/teen/your_mind/mental_health/suicide. html#cat20123

Youth Gambling Resources

- Connecticut Council on Problem Gambling, 16 West Main Street, Clinton, CT 06413, 188/789-7777
- The National Council on Problem Gambling, www.ncpgambling.org/, 730 11th St., NW, Ste 601, Washington, DC 20001, Phone 202-547-9204, Fax 202-547-9206
- Preventionlane, Lane County Prevention Program, http://prevention lane.org

- Arizona Office of Problem Gambling, Office of Problem Gambling, www.problemgambling.az.gov/, 1110 W Washington St., Suite 450, Phoenix, AZ 85007, 602-542-8998

- Connecticut Council on Problem Gambling, www.ccpg.org, 888-789-7777

- Colorado Department of Education, Exceptional Student Services Unit, www.cde.state.co.us, 201 E Colfax, Denver, CO 80203, 303-866-6694.

- Gama-teen Help, www.gama-teen.zoomshare.com/. For children of parents who gamble as well as those who have other family members who gamble

- Teen Gambling, www.teenhelp.com/teen-issues/teen-gambling.html

- Youth Gambling Is Not a Game, www.youtube.com/watch?v=KRBf7 zwDQrE

- Healthy People 2010, www.healthypeople.gov/

- MedlinePLUS Health Statistics, www.nlm.nih.gov/medlineplus/health statistics.html

- National Center for Health Statistics (NCHS), www.cdc.gov/nchs/.

Rape Resources

There are rape crisis centers in most cities. Check your phone directories or Google.

- Boston Area Rape Crisis Center, www.barcc.org/
- RAINN (Rape, Abuse and Incest National Network), www.rainn.org/
- Safehorizon, www.safehorizon.org/index/what-we-do-2/rape--sexual-assault-64.html?gclid=CMmr1eH7mLkCFWNxQgodwUcAKg

Sources

American Academy of Child and Adolescent Psychiatry (2008). "Facts for Families, Teen Suicide," www.aacap.org/AACAP/Families_and_Youth/Facts_for_Families/Facts_for_Families_Pages/Teen_Suicide_10.aspx.

American Foundation for Suicide Prevention, www.afsp.org/.

Arialdi, M. Miniño, M. P. H. (2010). *Mortality Among Teenagers Aged 12–19 Years: United States, 1999–2006.* NCHS Data Brief No. 37. Washington, DC: Centers for Disease Control and Prevention, www.cdc.gov/nchs/data/databriefs/db37.pdf.

Bilchik, S. (1999). "Promising Strategies to Reduce Gun Violence." Washington, DC: Department of Justice, Office of Justice Programs, Office of Juvenile Justice and Delinquency Prevention, www.ojjdp.gov/pubs/gun_violence/173950.pdf.

California Department of Motor Vehicles Driver Education, www.dmv.ca.gov/pubs/curriculum/.

Centers for Disease Control and Prevention (2012). "National Survey of Family Growth," www.cdc.gov/nchs/nsfg/key_statistics.htm.

Centers for Disease Control and Prevention (2013), "Parent–Teen Driving Contract," www.cdc.gov/motorvehiclesafety/teen_drivers/.

Centers for Disease Control and Prevention, National Center for Injury Prevention and Control, Division of Violence Prevention (2011). "Lesbian, Gay, Bisexual and Transgender Health," www.cdc.gov/lgbthealth/youth.htm.

Centers for Disease Control and Prevention, National Center for Injury Prevention and Control, Division of Violence Prevention (2013). "National

Suicide Statistics at a Glance," www.cdc.gov/violenceprevention/suicide/statistics/youth_risk.html.

Century Council, www.centurycouncil.org/underage-drinking/underage-drinking-research.

Confronting Electronic Bullying, www.sd36.bc.ca/earlma/documents/confronting_electronic_bullying.pdf.

Cyber Bullying: Statistics and Tips, www.isafe.org/outreach/media/media_cyber_bullying.

Davis, L. (2010). "An Educator's Guide to Children Affected by Parental Drug Abuse," eric.ed.gov/?id=EJ880897.

"Drunk Driving and Underage Drinking Data, Broken down by State" (2013), www.centurycouncil.org/blog/2013/drunk-driving-and-underage-drinking-data-broken-down-state.

Espelage, D., et al., (2011). *Classroom Violence Directed against Teachers.* Washington, DC: APA Board of Educational Affairs Task Force on Classroom Violence Directed Against Teachers, www.apa.org/ed/schools/cpse/activities/classroom-violence.aspx.

Fein, R.A. et al., *Threat Assessment in Schools: A Guide to Managing Threatening Situations and to Creating Safe School Climates.* Washington, DC: US Secret Service and US Department of Education, www.secretservice.gov/ntac/ssi_guide.pdf.

Glassbrenner, D. and Ye, T.J. (2007). NHTSA's National Center for Statistics and Analysis Traffic Safety Facts Research Note, National Highway Traffic Safety Administration, www-nrd.nhtsa.dot.gov/Pubs/810796.pdf.

Goldberg, C. (2013). "National Study: Teen Misuse and Abuse of Prescription Drugs Up 33 Percent Since 2008, Stimulants Contributing to Sustained Rx Epidemic." The Partnership at drugree.org, www.drugfree.org/newsroom/pats-2012.

Government of Alberta, Canada Transportation, Bus Safety Rules for Elementary School Students, www.cbe.ab.ca/policies/policies/AR6096.pdf.

Holmes, T.J. (2010). "Walking To School In A War Zone: A Look at School Violence in Chicago." *Huffington Post,* October 20, 2010, www.huffingtonpost.com/2010/10/20/walking-to-school-in-a-wa_n_770602.html.

Howell, J.C. and Decker, S.H. (1999). "The Youth Gangs, Drugs, and Violence Connection." US Department of Justice, Office of Justice Programs,

Office of Juvenile Justice and Delinquency Prevention, www.ncjrs.gov/pdffiles1/93920.pdf.

Insurance Institute for Highway Safety, www.iihs.org/research/topics/teenagers.html.

Michigan Parent–Teen Safe Driving Contract, www.michigan.gov/documents/DES_Parent-Teen_Safe_Driving_Contract_157407_7.pdf.

National Center on Addiction and Substance Abuse at Columbia University (2012). "National Survey of American Attitudes on Substance Abuse XVII: Teens," www.casacolumbia.org/upload/2012/20120822teensurvey.pdf.

National Domestic Abuse Hotline, www.loveisrespect.org, 1866-331-9474.

National Institute of Mental Health (2009). "New Approach to Reducing Suicide Attempts among Depressed Teens," www.nimh.nih.gov/news/science-news/2009/new-approach-to-reducing-suicide-attempts-among-depressed-teens.shtml.

National Suicide Prevention Lifeline and Crisis Line, 1800-784-2433 (1800-SUICIDE), www.suicidepreventionlifeline.org/.

"New Mexico Department of Health Data." *Albuquerque Journal,* November 19, 2011, p. C1.

No author (2011). *National Gang Threat Assessment: Emerging Trends.* Quantico, VA: FBI, www.fbi.gov/stats-services/publications/2011-national-gang-threat-assessment/2011-national-gang-threat-assessment-emerging-trends.

O'Toole, M. E. (2002). *The School Shooter: A Threat Assessment Perspective.* Quantico, VA: FBI, www.fbi.gov/stats-services/publications/school-shooter.

Our Lady of the Angels, December 1, 1958, www.olafire.com/FireSummary.asp.

Patchin, J.W. (March 21, 2013). "Cyberbullying: Neither an Epidemic nor a Rarity." Cyberbullying Research Center, http://cyberbullying.us/cyberbullying-neither-an-epidemic-nor-a-rarity/.

Policy Research Report #SRS2 (2000). *Are Zero Tolerance Policies Effective in the Schools?: An Evidentiary Review and Recommendations.* Washington, DC: APA and Zero Tolerance Task Force, www.apa.org/pubs/info/reports/zero-tolerance.pdf.

"Projected Smoking-Related Deaths Among Youth—United States" (1996). Centers for Disease Control and Prevention, www.cdc.gov/mmwr/preview/mmwrhtml/00044348.htm.

Robers, S., Zhang, J., and Truman, J. (2010). *Indicators of School Crime and Safety: 2010.* Washington, DC: National Center for Educational Statistics, US Department of Education and Bureau of Justice Statistics, Office of Justice Programs, US Department of Justice, http://nces.ed.gov/pubs2011/2011002.pdf.

Skiba, R. J. (2008). *Zero Tolerance, Zero Evidence: An Analysis of School Disciplinary Practice,* www.indiana.edu/~safeschl/ztze.pdf.

Substance Abuse and Mental Health Services Administration, www.samhsa.gov/.

Substance Abuse and Mental Health Services Association (n.d.). "There Are Many Reasons Why Children Start Drinking," http://samhsa.gov/underagedrinking/pdfs/why_children_start_drinking.pdf.

Temple, J. R. (2012.) "'Sexting' Common Among US Teens." Archives of Pediatric and Adolescent Medicine, www.primaryissues.org/2012/07/sexting-risky-behavior/.

University of Illinois at Urbana-Champaign, McKinley Health Center (2010). "What You Should Know About Sex & Alcohol," www.mckinley.illinois.edu/handouts/sex_alcohol.html.

US Department of Justice (2010). "National Drug Intelligence Center Releases National Drug Threat Assessment 2010," www.justice.gov/opa/pr/2010/March/10-ag-314.html.

"Why Do Adolescents Drink, What Are the Risks, and How Can Underage Drinking Be Prevented?" (2006). *Alcohol Alert* 67, http://pubs.niaaa.nih.gov/publications/AA67/AA67.htm.